EXILE

EXILE

A MODERN WILDERNESS JOURNEY

RANDALL L. CUMLEY

Exile: A Modern Wilderness Journey

Copyright © 2017 Randall Cumley

Published by Christian Book Press.

All rights reserved. No portion of this book may be reproduced in any form without permission from the publisher, except as permitted by U.S. copyright law.

ISBN: 978-1-948153-00-3

ACKNOWLEDGEMENTS

Robert and Maricia McMahon collaborated with God to set the stage for my journey through their generous gift of access to their home in Belize. That beautiful retreat on the Caribbean allowed me to escape the rat race of America, catch my breath and clear my view. The McMahon's knew before I did that God was at work in my life and they graciously supported His cause. For more than five years their gifts, encouragement and prayer formed a foundation for my journey. If this book impacts anyone's life, Bob and Maricia must share in the credit.

Steve Fisher paved the way for my trucking adventures starting with the oil field. Steve was my telephone confidant as we each covered thousands of miles crossing the nation in our individual trucks. He understood, more than anyone in my life, the ups and downs of life on the highway and was the person I could share with when no one else would have understood. With his signature good nature and a willingness to help wherever he can, Steve is a friend to everyone he meets and to be Steve's friend is to be blessed.

DEDICATION

To Mary: the woman who 'got it' long before I did and was willing to stay with me until I caught up. Mary's faith has anchored our family through the challenges of life for almost four decades. In the years when I was adrift, she held to the truth, securing us both, until God could get through to me. At times she lived her own exile parallel to mine. I pray we continue to be joined as one throughout eternity.

1

Through a tiny airplane window I could see the straight lines of runway lights marking our destination. The distinctive lights of the airport were surrounded on all sides by a sea of flickering city lights that revealed how big this town was becoming. A steady, five year stream of workers had expanded western North Dakota into a boom economy. Reluctantly, I was about to join the boom and become one of those workers.

Three months before, when Mary and I were making Christmas plans and pondering the approaching new year we would never have imagined North Dakota in the winter as a place for me to work, but there I was, landing at the Williston airport at 10 p.m. on a frigid night in February. Tiny flakes of windblown snow danced around the airplane as we taxied toward the terminal building. The plane lurched to a stop and we all sat silently for a moment until the familiar chime of the Captain turning off the fasten seat belt sign confirmed our arrival. As I stood in the narrow aisle of the plane, waiting for the line of passengers to exit, I tried to understand, or at least accept, the reality that I had run out of options and that lack of options had brought me to this bizarre point in life.

When I reached the cabin door and felt the cold night wind I realized my flannel lined jeans and winter parka were miserably inadequate for this environment. I pulled the parka tight around me, ducked my head to clear the cabin door, stepped down the folding stairs to the tarmac and walked briskly through light snow and strong wind to the terminal door.

A friend from the past was waiting inside. I had not seen Steve in person in almost eighteen years. We had reconnected six months ago when he popped up on my wife's Facebook feed. Driving a tanker truck in the Bakken oil field was going well for Steve and we had enjoyed following his oil field adventures. Mary and I were happy to see Steve was thriving in his second year in the oil field but, until three weeks ago, we never imagined I would join him as an oil field trucker.

Short exchanges over social media had grown into phone calls and now Steve and I were smiling and shaking hands in the baggage claim of a small, crowded, incredibly cold airport. Steve had arranged a job for me with his employer; a job I was not excited about or even interested in having but, for reasons I could not see or understand, this was my only option.

We loaded my two large suitcases into Steve's pickup truck and headed to Walmart. The clock on the dashboard said 10:25 p.m. but the town was full of activity. Williston had become a unique landscape of trucks that moved day and night. The streets were full of trucks, the parking lots were full of trucks and the air was filled with noise, and smoke and lights as trucks crisscrossed the town apparently unaware that this was the middle of a cold winter night and sensible people should be in bed.

The Walmart was crowded with men in work clothes buying food and supplies. The shelves were surprisingly disorganized and, in many areas, empty. Cardboard boxes littered the floors and pallets sat in the aisles. The Walmart staff had abandoned normal stocking practices because the products they brought out were snatched up by hurried shoppers before they could be placed on a shelf. Store employees had surrendered to the demand and pace of the oil boom by setting pallets in the aisles, removing the shrink wrap and letting the customers grab their purchase directly from the pallets.

Steve guided me through the store like an industrial version of a life coach introducing me to a new culture. Life as an oil field trucker has its own unique quirks and my coach was moving me quickly through the learning curve. His experience would leapfrog me past a lot of rookie mistakes, starting with what to stock up on for life lived inside a truck in a frozen land. After the Walmart experience, we drove thirty miles south on a crowded two-lane highway. Steve pointed out important landmarks and began my education about oil field culture.

Just before midnight we pulled into the company yard. A line of semi-trucks parked side by side covered the length of a football field with engines idling, their exhaust stacks puffing warm billows of smoke in the glow of overhead lights. The trucks rocked gently in the North Dakota wind as light snow blew over and around everything. The oil boom created conditions that required these trucks to be both work and home. Each truck housed a single occupant, relying on the diesel engine for both heat and power. The engines were always running to stay ahead of the cold outside. Through the winter months, the engines would never shut off. Without the engine running both the truck and its occupant would freeze in a few hours.

Steve parked in front of my new home, a fourteen-year-old Freightliner Classic, and left his pickup truck running. It seemed funny in the middle of this strange life event, but I was glad to see the Freightliner was blue, my favorite color, inside and out. Not the screaming yellow of the next truck over.

Even at midnight trucks were moving around, entering or leaving the parking lot, appearing and disappearing in the frozen darkness. We shoved my suitcases and Walmart bags inside the Freightliner, which was sitting with the engine idling and the heater blowing warm air. "The bathroom," he told me, "is inside the shop". Steve pointed at a large metal building with two giant doors on each end twenty yards across the gravel parking lot. He cautioned me, "Don't be slow in the morning. There is only one shower for more than thirty men living in this compound." I climbed the steps on the passenger side of the Freightliner and ducked inside then stood between the seats and surveyed my new reality. Steve said goodnight, closed the door and I sat down on the bunk; alone, not sure what to do next, and still wondering how my life had come to this place at this time. Feeling like I had hit bottom, I did not really understand what was ahead of me. I didn't realize my downhill slide was still in progress and the bottom would eventually be much lower than this.

The cab was warm, the rumble of the engine was soothing and I slept much better than I had anticipated. Barely six hours passed before a subconscious concern about getting a hot shower had me up and moving. Bundled against the coldest wind I had ever felt,

I crossed the dirt lot just before dawn and entered the giant metal building which turned out to be the mechanic shop. Two complete truck and trailer rigs could fit inside parked side by side. Shelves filled with parts and supplies lined one wall. A row of fifty-five gallon drums containing various oils and fluids relevant to operating trucks separated the two work bays. In the southeast corner of the building, I found the coveted bathroom. It was small, simple and dirty. Signs posted on the walls admonished the users to "clean up after yourself, your mother doesn't work here." The signs were clearly ineffective and the inevitable result of a single bathroom serving thirty oil field men was my greeting on the first morning.

Arrival on Friday night was two days sooner than I could actually start work but I would have a day to acclimate to the world of oil with Steve as my guide before he left on Sunday for a few days at home. Our tasks for the first day were to get me set up and oriented to the oil field life. We inspected my truck and then headed out to a nearby disposal facility where Steve showed me the basic operations of a vacuum tanker. We pulled wastewater from a giant storage tank and moved it to the disposal dock. He introduced me to the site personnel and explained some of the cultural norms.

Some parts of the Bakken have been producing oil for several years giving the facilities time to develop. In this part of the county, numerous disposal wells are competing for the income they can earn pumping wastewater back into the ground. Disposing of oil rig waste is a lucrative business and the disposal companies know it is usually the tanker driver's choice of where they haul their water. The disposal facilities offer perks to the drivers as an enticement to choose one facility over another. This particular disposal has two nice restrooms with hot showers that are free for drivers who bring their wastewater here. They also offer an assortment of free food. It's all convenience store food, wrapped in plastic, like sandwiches, burritos and snacks to be warmed in the microwave. Endless pots of hot coffee and even soft drinks are offered to the drivers in this developed part of the oil boom. I would soon discover that I wouldn't be working in this area.

The roads there and back were crowded with trucks, trucks and more trucks. Two lane roads were struggling to carry the traffic loads that an oil boom had thrust upon the region. Every store or truck stop or parking lot was packed with trucks and men in work clothes. Hooded heads bowed and turned aside from the cutting wind as the workers stepped carefully over icy parking lots. Walking quickly from parking lot to store and back, the men moved like ants searching for supplies. After a brief tour of the town, we fueled the truck and returned to the shop. Steve wished me well as he loaded a month's worth of dirty laundry from his Kenworth into his pickup truck. Beneath the dull gray clouds of a winter sky, he pulled out for his eight-hour drive home to Minnesota.

That evening I discovered a gravel lot filled with idling trucks in the North Dakota winter was not a place for social interaction. Hidden within the steel cabs we were two and a half dozen men making the best we could of a life away from home. Each man living alone in a six-by-eight foot, diesel-heated, private retreat on wheels. Inside the equipment shop, there was an area referred to as a driver lounge that had two old couches and two old truck seats. A dining room table with one broken leg leaned against the wall in the corner. A microwave oven sat on the table beside a nearly empty bottle of ketchup and some plastic single-serving mustard packets. This room was just as dirty as the shared bathroom. There was no television but the room had the strongest Wi-Fi signal on the property. The driver's lounge was empty when I looked around so I decided to eat in my truck.

For dinner the first night I had a microwave gourmet of fried chicken from the grocery store deli and potato salad eaten straight from the plastic deli container while sitting on the bunk inside the truck. I unpacked my suitcases into the storage compartments of my mobile motel room, loaded groceries into the small refrigerator and made the bed.

As the sun rose on Sunday morning I was sitting alone in an oil field truck wondering if the wind would ever stop blowing and if the temperature would make it up to freezing today. The shop mechanics had a small SUV in the parking lot they used to go get parts. On weekends, the beat up little wreck was available to drivers for running short errands. I pushed the trash and cigarette butts aside just enough to get into the driver's seat and headed to town in search of breakfast. A half an hour later I was back at the shop with a cup of truck stop coffee and a plastic wrapped muffin that I consumed while sitting in the passenger seat of my truck. Day two of "I don't know what I've gotten into" was off to a slow and miserable start. Steve was gone for the week leaving me like a fish out of water in a land I didn't know surrounded by a culture I didn't understand. I spent the day searching for enough mental focus to read a book in hopes I could ignore the growing depression threatening to drown my soul. With that much time to kill, it was inevitable that I would begin to dissect how I had ended up here.

Oil field truck driver was not my identity. I knew myself as an entrepreneur, a businessman, a creator and risk taker. New ideas, developed into reality, had been my life. The previous decade I owned and operated a thriving small business supporting highway construction in Colorado. I had a life of relative comfort with income and options including my own small airplane which I piloted for business and pleasure. My family vacationed frequently with several trips each year to our favorite places in the Caribbean. My life was filled with the perks and privilege of being a business owner.

Employees handled the daily details, leaving me to manage business functions like bidding on work, negotiating contracts and overseeing accounts. I set my own schedule and could come and go as I pleased. I was the boss and my decisions determined the direction of the company. That life now seemed long ago and so far away.

The economic crash of 2008 hit the construction industry very hard. Private work dried up entirely as every form of building construction abruptly halted. The lack of project financing shut down the real estate and construction boom that had been fueling middle-class American businesses. Every contractor and business that had the rug pulled out from under them in private projects rushed to the public sector where the federal government was shouting about "shovel ready projects." My business was built entirely around government-funded highway construction projects. This intense, new competition from so many businesses leaving the dead private market and pouring into the public sector tore the bottom out of our industry. Prices for services collapsed overnight. New competitors were hungry to enter the field and old competitors were desperate to generate cash flow, even at an overall loss. Through the course of 2009, we were bidding projects at prices that would not cover costs. The thought on everyone's mind was that small losses could be carried for a short time until this all blew over. The optimism being floated out from Washington D.C. was encouraging the masses to hold on. Washington, they assured us, would fix this.

Exile: A Modern Wilderness Journey

We watched bid after bid fail to land a new project, even at cost or below. I refused to go into debt just to maintain a death spiral. I decided to close the business and take a break. We finished the current contracts, laid off our employees, and put equipment in storage. I was not rich enough to retire, but I could afford to take some time away from work at a relatively young age. I decided to call this a sabbatical.

Along with shutting down my business, the crashing economics of 2008 also triggered my interest in Central America as the place for either a potential new business or an early retirement. Maybe becoming a snowbird would be an option. Many hours of Internet study brought Belize to the forefront as the country of best options. Mary and I booked a week-long trip to explore this tiny, English-speaking country. In early 2010 I made several more trips on my own, each a bit longer and more in-depth as my interest in Belize increased. I began to make friends among the retirees and adventurers who had already made their move to a small strip of land along the southeastern coast. I fell in love with the geography, the warm winter temperature and the attitude of the entire community.

The owners of a guest house where I stayed on my first visit became close friends. On my third trip in as many months, they asked if I would be willing to care for their three suite guest house while they took an extended visit to the U.S. What great luck! This gave me free lodging in a fantastic home on the edge of the Caribbean Ocean for two and half months. In June, I went home to Colorado and tried to sort out the opportunity that seemed to be unfolding. By the end of the summer, the owners of that beautiful guest house on the beach decided to move permanently to the U.S. and offered to turn my house sitting into a long term arrangement. I could keep my clothes and personal belongings in the owner's residence upstairs and would come and go at will. When I was in Belize I would manage the property and live upstairs. They received the income from the rental suites to supplement their fixed income in the states and I got free housing in Belize. My new life was taking shape but if this was going to last I needed an income.

Real estate was booming in this retirement and vacation mecca. Research was screaming that building homes to sell would be a viable business. I had a strong background in construction and had built homes before. The guest house I was caring for was in a neighborhood of homes and empty building lots. The expensive homes were on the beach and the affordable lots were across the street. We bought a building lot across the street from the beach to keep the cost of the house within our target price range. The lot was not right on the ocean but we could see the water and feel the breeze. My new business, building houses, would soon be underway.

Returning to Colorado to tie up some loose ends, I advertised all of my highway construction equipment for sale. Sale flyers were mailed and faxed to former competitors who were still fighting to stay alive. The chance to pick up specialized equipment at fire sale prices was an opportunity for them. Everything sold in a few short weeks except one pickup truck I held back. I would ship that to Belize, loaded with tools, to be my construction work truck. Mary would hold down the Colorado homestead while I established a new business in Belize.

My goal was to be very hands-on and involved in the construction process. I needed to test some techniques that were common in the states, but new to Central American builders. I hired two local men as my full-time laborers and made friends with a local contractor who was willing to help when we needed bigger crews for certain tasks. This would be a modest house aimed at the middle price range of the real estate market. I learned how to build the Belizean way which depends on labor rather than equipment. The work was physically exhausting in a hot and humid climate that was like nothing I had ever experienced. I had never in my life been so tired, so dirty and so drenched in sweat and yet, in spite of the exhaustion, the challenge was exhilarating.

Working alongside the men I hired taught me the methods common to Belize while I showed them some of the tools and techniques from the states. Genuine friendships developed with more than a few of the locals. They started to invite me to their homes in small, very poor villages a few miles inland where I learned about local life in a third world village.

These people worked harder than anyone I had ever seen but their work produced only enough income each day to survive another day. Here the phrase, *"if you don't work you don't eat"* was literal. These skilled and loyal craftsmen could barely provide for their family. They worked in the rain. They worked in the heat. They worked sixty hours every week whether they were healthy or sick. They worked carefully because getting hurt would mean no work and no work would lead to hunger and homelessness for themselves and their family. There were no social safety nets. No insurance, no unemployment benefits and no disability programs. All they seemed to have were long days of hard labor in a searing hot sun. I had never lived so close to or experienced a life so barren. Exposure to the hard life of the locals left me wondering why anyone would work this hard day after day when it was clear they had no chance of getting ahead. Viewed from my American perspective, what I saw was that they had no opportunity to accomplish anything beyond mere survival day after day until they died. I wrestled with the question: Why would they continue such hard, apparently meaningless lives? If life was nothing more than subsisting for eighty years, why not just quit? I then had to process what my soul was exploring with the thought, why not just quit? How can anyone quit life? The question began growing in the back of my mind as I pushed forward on the house.

My idea of a house construction business had started in November and an architect was hired with the goal of starting work immediately after the first of the year. Belize soon taught me that nothing happens fast in a Caribbean country. Actual construction did not begin until May and by the following March the project had been dragging on too long. Without income, our expenses were eating up our savings and our backup investments had gone the wrong direction. I was deep into a project that was progressing slowly and burning cash. I had to close up the house, park the truck and head back to Colorado in search of a means to finish this.

Networking through contacts uncovered a possible job as a project manager for a large residential and resort project which, amazingly, was in Belize. This could be perfect. The property was barely a hundred yards north of my Belize house. They said they were in the final stages of financing and would be ready to break ground in sixty days or less. Working over the phone and the internet from my home in the U.S., I invested unpaid time and energy on preliminary development plans for the project as my way to demonstrate to them my project management skills. The resort company made a preliminary job offer, contingent on final financing commitments to the project. I had found my way forward.

That was almost a year ago and their project was still unfunded. Steve had told me oil field work was good income with no long term commitment. I came to the Bakken as a short term plan to pay our bills until the big project in Belize could finalize their funding and call me to work.

2

The other drivers moved in and out of the yard at all hours of the day and night headed to or coming from assignments I did not yet understand. Joining the procession of trucks was not an option for me until I completed a required drug screen Monday morning.

As the owner of my own business, I had never been subjected to an employment drug test. When the medical clinic opened at 8 a.m., I joined a dozen other rookie drivers in the less than glamorous process of a federally mandated drug screen. When I left the small medical clinic that was now making a fortune processing plastic vials of urine; I explored the small town that was clearly overwhelmed by the oil boom and in transition. Store fronts that had been boarded up five years before were once again open, attempting to supply the needs oil field workers. Restaurants accustomed to feeding an agricultural community now struggled to serve the rough and sometimes rowdy clientele of an oil boom. Throughout the town trucks of all types constantly moved around in a chaotic dance of noise and smoke.

Back at the shop, I waited for the drug test results to be faxed to the company office. I met a few of the mechanics in the shop, filled out new hire paperwork and wondered how I was going to live life in a truck, supported by a filthy bathroom. A long and lonely day was spent mostly inside the truck trying to read or nap. Around 9 p.m. I was just beginning to think of crawling into bed when my isolation was broken by someone pounding on the side of the truck. Dreading the cold air, I cracked open the passenger side window just enough to hear a burly, coverall encrusted man whose name I don't know shout over the wind: "They want you in the office." Climbing down from the truck I pulled my parka close against the cold night and trudged to the big metal building. I had hoped to get a good night of sleep and that didn't seem to be where this was headed.

In the office, I was introduced to my trainer and informed we were headed out for a night shift. The temperature was zero and the wind was at least twenty five mph. A multi-colored wind chill chart on the office wall showed the combined wind chill as minus twenty-four Fahrenheit. The dispatcher observed out loud that the coat I had on was not going to keep me warm at these temps. He offered me a heavy work parka left behind by the last driver who couldn't take this life and disappeared in the night. Apparently that was a common way for drivers to end their tenure here. Salvaged from the personal items that driver had left inside his truck when he cut and ran, this flame resistant, OSHA approved parka was two sizes too big but it was better than what I brought. The dispatcher wanted seventy dollars from me for this coat he got for free. He was willing to wait until my first paycheck to get his money. I returned to my truck and drove up to the office to begin my first night of oil field trucking.

My trainer was another driver currently on light duty with an ankle injury. He climbed into my truck and gave basic directions to get us started toward the assignment. This would be a "flow-back" and we would be hauling wastewater coming out of a completed fracking operation. Danny appeared to be in his sixties, a bit overweight, dressed lightly considering the weather, friendly and talkative. He did not ask before lighting his first cigarette in my truck. I made a mental note to get a no smoking sign for the dash.

Forty minutes of two-lane highway brought us to the top of a hill where Danny directed me to turn off the pavement onto a dirt road. At 10:15 p.m. the road was almost bumper to bumper with slow-moving trucks crawling along in a continuous line of lights in both directions. We were entering a Native American reservation cooperatively owned by three tribes. Once a desolate home for the outcasts of America's expansion, this land now gushed wealth through hundreds of wells pulling oil from a mile beneath the surface. The glow of gas flares reflected off the clouds overhead like an orange ceiling above the white flood lights on every hill side. Record high oil prices had pushed every available drill rig and exploration company into the Bakken. The assortment of truck mounted equipment needed to support the drilling defied imagination.

A highway sign before the turn had identified this as Road 12. Light snow was blowing horizontally across the headlights as we crawled along the roughest dirt road I had ever driven on. The truck would bounce and bang through ruts and potholes. I tried to weave around the roughest spots that could be seen in the headlights but occasionally we would slam down hard when the tires broke through the thin ice of frozen puddles that I couldn't see in the dark. Fourteen miles on this road took an hour to cover then Danny pointed and grunted, sucking on his third cigarette, signaling me to turn right onto a paved two-lane road.

Two miles of winding pavement barely wide enough for the string of trucks passing each other in both directions carried us over several hills. The lights of drilling rigs were visible on hilltops and down in valleys in every direction. "Start slowing down," Danny told me. With another cigarette glowing in his hand, he pointed at a gate in the wire fence, ahead on the right. "Turn there and gear down for the hill," he said. Following his instructions, the truck was barely off the pavement when I slammed on the brakes. The headlights were shining through the night sky illuminating another hillside a quarter mile away. Below the headlights, through the darkness in front of the truck bumper I could barely see a narrow gravel road that dove steeply down an ice covered hill. A mile ahead and two hundred feet below at the end of this winding road the flood lights of a well pad illuminated the maze of activity that is a fracking site.

"What's wrong, " Danny asked. "You can't drive a truck down that hill," I told him, shaking my head in wonder. My adult life had taken me through several variations of employment usually involved in some form of construction. Whether building homes or amusement parks or highways, construction had been the primary theme of my life and that included trucks. My first commercial driver's license was a badge of honor to an eighteen-year-old. Throughout adult life, the ability to drive any rig was a convenient skill to have in my back pocket. Sometimes operating a truck helped my business, and other times it was a fallback skill that paid the bills between jobs. I had never been a true professional trucker, but I did have some experience as a driver. That experience was telling me this road was not a safe option for a truck of this size.

"We've been driving this road all week," Danny said. I looked over at his grin. I could see he enjoyed bringing rookies out on their first run. As I asked for his recommendation on how to handle this road that I thought was unsafe, a loaded truck roared up the hill toward us and disappeared into the darkness behind me. "Third gear, easy with the throttle and no matter what, don't touch the brakes," Danny told me as he lit another cigarette and set his muddy boots on the dashboard where that no smoking sign would soon be.

Three hours later my first load of fracking waste had been unloaded at the disposal and I was back at the well pad. Danny caught a ride from the disposal with another driver headed back to the shop and I was on my own. Apparently, one pass through the maze of a fracking site was all the training a rookie would get. From here on my education would be on the job and self-guided.

From Steve I had learned that disposing of frack water is an expense to the crude oil process. Our loads were measured as "barrels" which is another way of saying forty-two gallons. Every barrel of crude an oil tanker hauls away is income to the operation. Every barrel of water we haul off is an expense that eats away the profits. Water haulers are a necessary evil doing a dirty job in horrible conditions. Everyone out here knows that a water hauler is the lowest of the low in the oil field.

For the second time tonight I parked among a maze of pipes, hoses and tanks that were collecting and storing wastewater flowing out of the fracked well. Procedures required me to remain outside at the rear of the truck during the half hour it would take for the vacuum pump to pull four thousand gallons of fracking waste into my tanker. For safety, I was required to be where I could monitor the tank gauge. Overfilling the tank would create a hazardous waste spill which would earn no points in my favor with anyone. My clothing layers of thermal underwear and denim jeans under insulated coveralls were topped with the heavy parka I had gotten from the dispatcher. A fireproof hood covered my head under an OSHA required plastic hard hat. Leather work gloves protected my hands from the wind and the wastewater but I had been told the gloves would soon be too wet to wear and too filthy to take off. I was not freezing, but I was certainly not warm. The wind had increased along with the snow which was now thick and moving horizontally across the beams of light cast by trucks, equipment and light towers around the well pad. The earth vibrated under my feet from the dozens of diesel engines operating all the equipment that supported this operation. This many giant engines must be loud, but I could not hear anything over the howl of the wind. The red arrow on a large thermometer, securely mounted to the side of the pump building, pointed at minus twenty-two. The rig hand watching me load yelled through the wind that he just checked the computers inside. The wind chill was minus thirty-seven degrees Fahrenheit and it was 2 a.m. on a Tuesday in a North Dakota winter.

My mind wandered to February one year ago when I was scuba diving off the coast of Cozumel in crystal clear waters. With my back to this biting North Dakota wind, I remembered that I owned a house in Belize which was supposed to be the start of a new life where winter does not exist. At that moment I had clothes hanging in a closet sixty feet from the warm water's edge. My flip-flops waited by the door. But I was not there to use those clothes or those flip-flops. I was here in North Dakota in the middle of a howling blizzard at night because I needed a job and this was the only option I had been able to land. This was as far away from the life I desired, the life I had been living, as I could get. Like a punch to the gut I was hit by the realization: "I am in exile." In that nanosecond of comprehension my thought was immediately answered by the clear and unmistakable voice of God. Through the wind and the clothing and the dismay He instantly responded to my revelation with a warm and smiling, "Yes, you are."

3

My tanker was full, the rig hand started closing valves and I needed to get out of the way of the next truck. After securing my heavy rubber hoses, I climbed into the cab and began slowly driving through the maze of equipment toward that icy hill Danny had found so amusing. His words echoed in my mind: "No matter what, don't stop on the hill. You'll never get going again." The truck crawled up the winding road through blowing snow as my mind retraced every detail that could turn this into a major hassle. Going too slow I would lose the momentum needed to climb the hill. Too fast and I might slide off one of the half dozen curves in the narrow road. Shifting gears on the steep hill was not an option with this much weight. I have to be in the right gear at the right speed with enough momentum to get up the hill, over the crest and onto flat land and pavement.

Randall L. Cumley

When all eighteen wheels were back on asphalt, my thoughts switched to the road ahead. The disposal for this foul water was twenty four miles away. The trip would include another trek across that fourteen mile stretch of dirt no one outside the oil field would call a road. That was the fourth trip of the night over the string of ruts, rocks and potholes that is the only way to get trucks in and out of these wells. The wind continued to rock the truck but the snow had lightened up slightly. That orange glow in the sky, the reflection of a thousand gas flares on the clouds, concealed any signs of the dawn that must be approaching. Time of day seemed to be irrelevant in the oil field, and it looked like nothing ever stopped moving out here. Alone in the cab, I chose some solid paced music for the stereo and settled in for the rough crawl in a line of trucks out to the highway while I tried to understand what had just happened.

The concept of a direct and personal relationship with God was not new to my world. I was raised in a Bible belt church and I knew all the standard Sunday school stories. I could say grace at Thanksgiving dinner as well as the next guy and I knew most of the words to common Baptist hymns. In college, I took the usual wandering off track from my mother's religion but found my way back through marriage to a sweet and faithful young woman. Newly converted from Catholicism, she introduced me to the evangelic church and guided me into a believer's life. We raised two sons in protestant non-denominational churches where she and I both served as volunteer leaders. We even had a two-year stint as staff members living on site at a Christian camp operated by a national campus ministry. I had known about God all my life but it seemed I may have just met Him in person for the first time.

Exile: A Modern Wilderness Journey

I had felt God's voice in my soul actually speaking discernible words. Not only was He speaking, but my life was upside down, everything was wrong, I was in exile and God seemed to be amused. I was pretty sure He was grinning when He confirmed my revelation about exile.

When the sun finally rose Tuesday morning over the snow-covered hills I caught my first view of the area I had traversed multiple times in darkness. This was the rolling hills of the Great Plains, formerly home of buffalo and the wind. Only the wind remained. The area we were working in had almost no homes. A handful of cattle grazed on the brown winter grass. Less than a hundred permanent residents lived nearby in a small town that was strictly off limits to trucks. Our route out to the highway could have avoided the terrible fourteen miles of Road 12 except the only alternative was a paved road running through the small town. I understood why they did not want their town destroyed by this much truck traffic.

My assignment had started at 9 p.m. Monday night, stretched through the entire day on Tuesday and continued into Tuesday night. The system was simple enough. Load at the well pad. Grind along the fourteen miles of Road 12 out to the main highway for a ten-mile run to the disposal. Twenty minutes to pump the wastewater off at the disposal then head back to the well for another load. Settling into the three-hour round trip, I carried load after load of fracking waste off the reservation out to the disposal and then went back for more. Eight loads in twenty-four hours, sixteen bone-jarring journeys over Road 12, and there I was back at 9 p.m. with no indication when this would end.

I began to recognize a few of the other trucks from my company driving this loop but I knew none of the drivers' names. No one ever seemed to be at the same place at the same time even though I was sure at least some of them were working the same flow-back I was on. There was the red Kenworth with the giant front bumper they call a buffalo catcher. He had a lot of chrome and the truck seemed too nice to be out on these roads. The blue International was driven by a dark-haired man with a full beard who seemed to always be smiling. He waved whenever we passed in opposite directions. He drove fast, apparently oblivious to the conditions of Road 12, almost flying over the potholes and ruts. Twice in twenty-four hours he sailed past me as I slowed down to crawl through a particularly rough stretch of road. I wondered if his method of skimming the bumps was better or worse than the technique everyone else used, slowly picking our way through the potholes. My mind started crunching the numbers to see how much more money he would make if he hauled just two more loads per day than I did and if maybe that justified the kidney damage of his method.

Painted metal signs, like real estate for sale signs, at each well entrance displayed the name of the pad along with a numerical identity code. I was hauling flow-back from the Brown Bear well. Flow-back was what we called the waste water removed from the well in the final stage of the fracking process. The water and chemicals that had been pumped into the well to open up the shale were released and allowed to flow back out of the well to be hauled away. When a flow-back starts, the process can't be stopped. The parade of trucks had to be continuous day and night to keep up with the flow of waste coming out of the well. Leading and directing the truck operation is a man called the pusher. His job was to keep pushing the trucks and keep us all moving. Any issues we had, like lack of sleep, no food and no bathroom within fifty miles are of no concern to the pusher.

He cared only about maintaining the flow of trucks to remove the wastewater coming out of that well. We would be here as long as the water continued to flow.

Driving, loading, driving, unloading, I learned the rhythm of the oil field. Nothing was normal in any sense of normal that would be understood outside the industry. And yet, nothing was really unusual in the life of those who lives and worked here. "Whatever it takes to keep the oil flowing," was the mantra. What would be called an accident back in civilization was a non-event out here. A truck sliding off the road and tipping over was so normal as to be nearly ignored. The first few trucks behind an accident would make sure the driver was okay then return to their own truck and continue on. The driver whose truck was now lying on its side would make a few phone calls to start his own rescue. Within a few hours, his wrecked truck would be removed and he would be driving a different truck. During the process of removing the wrecked truck, every other truck would drive around the wreck and keep moving. Occasionally a truck would blow up or catch on fire, a few people would hit it with portable fire extinguishers and make sure the driver was safe. Everyone else would just keep moving. By the end of the day, the burnt out truck would be gone and through it all the oil field never stopped its rhythm or slowed its pace.

My smartphone was loaded with the music I had played as a nearly constant background to my life over the previous thirty years. The island theme of artists like Jimmy Buffet and his backup band the Coral Reefers had been an undertone behind nearly l everything I had done in my adult life. Suddenly, for no reason I could explain, my taste in music changed dramatically. Christian praise music became the only music I could tolerate. I tried to listen to the old secular favorites but they had no appeal. Of the two dozen albums I had loaded on my phone for this adventure, only four became my constant companions.

We were so far from civilization that music on the radio was not available. The only AM station in the area played Navajo drums and chanting. There were no FM stations in range and the cell signal was too weak in most places to get internet music. As my only option, those four Christian albums played over and over as the day turned into night and back to day again. The music provided a background for the flood of thoughts running through my mind. I dissected the previous year looking for reasons to explain how I ended up in this alternate reality.

Almost exactly one year ago I had returned from Belize pondering why the locals continued their subsistence life. I began intently searching for a deeper understanding of life, triggered by that experience with the locals. The simple question about why continue a subsistence life had grown into a hunger for truth unlike any pursuit I had ever known. Our small household library had a few books about heaven and the meaning of life. I started with those, and then moved to books recommended by friends. I read book after book looking for an explanation of why we all exist. Even though I had proclaimed through most of my life that I was a Christian, this was the clearest, most in-depth search I had ever pursued. The more I searched the more I realized the Bible studies I had participated in over the years had been little more than academic exercises. This search for understanding was turning into a quest that was personal and genuine. For some reason those hard-working third-world laborers had exposed a void in my soul that I needed to understand.

Over the previous year, while waiting for the resort job to start and watching our savings disappear; I had invested my spare time in hours of reading which turned into days of questions leading to weeks of study in a dozen books by as many authors. For almost a year, I had been wrestling with a desire to understand life that was bigger than anything I had ever experienced. This was becoming the most driven and committed pursuit of meaning I had ever known. And none of that connected, in any way that I could see, with hauling wastewater in a North Dakota winter.

The first four days and three nights slid by in an endless loop as I hauled flow-back from the Brown Bear well until the pusher told me this was my last load. The flow-back was ending and he was cutting trucks. After taking this load to the disposal I could head to town for fuel, a hot shower in that filthy bathroom and a long sleep.

The demand for trucks throughout the Bakken far exceeded the supply of trucks available. Priority in assigning trucking resources went to the operations that carried highly valuable crude oil from the wells into shipping terminals. The drivers who moved crude oil could work no more than twelve hours before turning their truck over to another driver. This rule was implemented to protect the valuable oil. When they weren't moving oil, crude oil drivers lived in houses or apartments in town or in campers at hastily built RV parks called man camps. All of the housing options in a boom town were expensive and when utilities and transportation costs were added in the local cost of living was astronomical.

Water haulers were the opposite of crude oil drivers. There was a limited supply of trucks assigned to moving water and safety was low on the list of priorities. We were carrying a waste product that had no value and we were an expense for the oil companies. Using fewer resources we could only manage the task of wastewater disposal by ignoring both common sense and federal safety laws. The small companies and rogue independents hauling water worked insane hours because the money at stake overpowered the risks.

The only way to work that many hours was to live in our trucks which meant we paid no rent and no utilities so our cost of living was minimal. We were not limited to established work shifts and water haulers would drive for days and days with very little sleep. A nap of two to three hours each day was the most sleep a water hauler could get when an operation was in progress. After four or six or even eight days of nearly continuous work the drivers would collapse in fatigue when released from their assignment. Drivers did not complain about the long hours because the continuous day and night work generated big income. Living in the truck was the only way all of this craziness could take place.

Inside the cab of my Freightliner, behind the seats, the ceiling of the truck was high enough I could stand and stretch my arms to a skylight overhead. Immediately behind the passenger seat I had a small refrigerator bolted to the floor. A microwave oven was strapped to the top of the refrigerator. Cabinets attached to the wall above the microwave held my groceries. On the opposite side, behind the driver seat, a cabinet on the floor stored bottled water, coats, gloves and hats. The top of that cabinet served as a nightstand for the bed. Above that, on the wall behind the driver seat, another cabinet held clean, dry clothing and my doughnut stash. A full-sized bed stretched the full width across the back of the cab. Power inverters provided electricity to run the refrigerator, the microwave and small appliances like a coffee maker. Each driver loaded the inside of his truck with the comforts he preferred. Many had a television and DVD player to watch movies when there was no driving. We all carried enough food and spare clothing to meet our needs for at least several days, if not weeks. Other than what we carried in our trucks, there were no resources available on the reservation to support our life.

Steve worked on the opposite side of the county where the drivers lived a very different life. Two years in the Bakken made him a senior driver and took him to assignments a rookie like me could not get. We spoke on the phone every few days and his description of life fifty miles to the west sounded luxurious. The amenities and services available to drivers on his side of the county had developed over time in the area of the Bakken where drilling had begun several years prior. The eastern fields, where I was working, were just now in the process of being opened up. Consistently high oil prices and strong demand were pushing oil companies to drill and open wells faster than the supporting infrastructure could be built. Here in the sparsely populated land of the reservation we had no showers, no stores and no amenities. The water disposals where we dumped our waste, were hastily built, bare-bones operations on gravel lots operated from temporary office trailers. We were a world apart from the mature fields further west.

On most assignments, I could operate three to four days before the truck needed fuel, which was only available in town. The hour plus drive back to the civilization of a small town fuel station was my opportunity to do laundry, catch a shower and buy groceries. There were two washing machines and two dryers at the company shop, right outside the filthy bathroom. Too many men had washed too many greasy and oily clothes in these machines. Everything came out looking clean and feeling okay, but the freshly laundered clothes always smelled like diesel fuel. While at the office I could drop off invoices and paperwork, and then drive to the grocery store to restock food supplies.

When there was no work, sometimes for several days, many drivers would wait at the shop, confined by the wind to a life lived inside their idling trucks. They spent hours watching sports or old movies. My preference was to stock up on fuel and supplies and get back to the field. There was no money to be made at the shop. Camping out on the reservation, even on non-work days, kept me close to where the work was. When a new assignment cropped up, or if a truck working an assignment broke down, I was the closest available truck to step in. This approach brought me more work, but it also kept me isolated out in the wilderness. I used the time camping and waiting to read, nap, listen to music and try to find an understanding of why my life had wound down to this.

Tucked away on a remote well pad, removed from distractions, I had time to retrace my studies of the previous year. I remembered it was Steve's wife who had suggested, in a social media post, that a certain book by N.T. Wright should be read by any serious Christ follower. The book, *Surprised by Hope*, was on sale that week, only $3.99 for e-readers, so I downloaded it. My e-reader was here in the truck and I opened the book again. Bishop Wright's presentation of life after death disputed everything my upbringing had planted in my brain. That book completely changed my thoughts about what eternity will be and it sent me in search of more information. A drastically new understanding of heaven exploded my prior beliefs and added to my still unfolding spiritual inquiry. The questions bouncing around inside my brain were not directly from Bishop Wright's book, but the view of an afterlife on a redeemed earth that he presented was mixing in with the questions from Belize in a thought process that was re-arranging my core beliefs.

There was plenty of time to revisit the previous year's studies as the key word to describe my life in the Bakken was isolation. I was alone for hours and days and weeks. There were other drivers coming and going but very little time for conversation, not that I had anything to say or was in any mood to talk. At times when there might be two or three drivers together at a well pad or a disposal, the noise of the equipment prevented conversation. If we weren't driving alone, we were outside, in the weather, loading or unloading wastewater. Outside the truck, we were surrounded by the noise of diesel engines and screaming pumps. Most days we had no chance to connect with another human beyond a nod and a smile.

When there was water to be moved it often was paid by the load, not by the hour. The number of loads hauled in a day would determine the income for that day. The income was good when a project was running but the opportunity to earn was a perishable commodity that had to be harvested when it was ripe. Projects would come and go constantly with little or no advance notice. Most assignments lasted only a few days at a time and during those days the pressure to keep moving was intense. Stopping to sleep could cause a huge loss of income. A driver could wake up from a long rest to discover the project had ended while he was snoring.

Whenever I could take a break on a hilltop within range of a cell tower I would call home and check in with Mary. Most days she would send random text messages which were my lifeline. I didn't want to talk to anyone else back home in my previous life for many reasons. I refused to accept in my own mind the idea that I was no longer a successful entrepreneur. Talking about this steep life decline with friends or family by revealing, and thereby admitting, that I was nothing more than a water hauler in a barren wasteland was too much humility to face. Subconsciously I was hoping this would be a very, very short exile and perhaps I could glide through this whole experience unseen by anyone outside the oil field. I was alone in a truck with no one to talk to, except God. I began to discover, for the first time in my life, what it meant to have conversations with God.

Those conversations were short and unpredictable. Our relationship seemed to have a narrow focus. I asked simple, sincere questions and God gave short, direct answers, usually in four words or less, delivered with a smile that was palpable. There were no dissertations from either of us.

That first night God had confirmed my revelation that this was exile. The exact opposite of where I thought my life should be going. I had a Bible and a laptop with me so I searched for an understanding of what exile meant. From the fundamentalist church of my youth I carried a vision of exile as punishment. My belief system held that bad people were carried off into exile in response to their sinful lives. "Had my life been so bad," I asked out loud, "to deserve this?"

The hours of tedious driving gave me plenty of time to ponder how the idea of exile as a punishment could be applied to my current situation. With time to look back at my recent history, I could not deny that the successful years of owning a business had led me to a life of consumerism that ignored God.

At first, it was the intense demands of starting a new business that kept me out of church. If the business was going to survive I had to be on the highway Sunday mornings moving equipment between job sites to set up the coming week. Bookkeeping and reporting in the evenings replaced church board meetings and covering for missing employees took the place of lunches with the pastor. I quickly abandoned my church life and lost touch with the church family.

As the business grew and the money flowed in, I began to accumulate toys. Looking back at life from the cab of that truck, I had to admit I really missed my airplane. Of all the perks that business provided, flying my own single-engine plane was the best. I would have given almost anything for the opportunity to once again soar over the Rocky Mountains with my family on board headed for a weekend at the lake. I missed the vacations and I missed the travel. The job of owner required every ounce of mental energy to get through the primary building season but, when winter weather brought a slowdown to highway construction, I traveled to warm beaches for scuba diving by day and fine food and drink at night. I truly loved a good hotel with a giant bed covered in fine sheets and piles of pillows. I remembered warm winter days reading a good book by the pool sipping an umbrella drink or snacking on food at the pool-side bar. In almost every way we had achieved the American Dream. Now the airplane and all the other toys were gone. I had nothing left from the business but an unfinished house in a foreign country I could not afford to visit.

5

Day after day, life in the Bakken rumbled slowly by in an endless slog of tedious driving on bad roads in bad weather. Some drivers were less motivated than others, more resigned to being out there long-term and simply grinding out a living. Others, like myself, had hopes of making a pile of money and getting out as quickly as possible. I learned that the long-term grind it out guys preferred to drive daylight hours, not work too much, and sleep at night. This meant the opportunity for greatest income was through the night and early morning hours. During daylight hours, too many trucks were on site, competing for a load, waiting in long lines of idling trucks. A driver might sit for two to three hours waiting a turn to get a load. The day shift might only provide two or three payloads in twelve hours, but at night the grind it out drivers disappeared. Those of us who stayed could pull into the loading station with no waiting, load immediately, race to the disposal site and hustle back for another payload. Income doubled at night and there was a bonus of no DOT officers checking weights. We were paid according to how many barrels we could move. Running heavy increased the pay but it was too risky during the day as the fines for being caught overweight could wipe out a week's income.

The sweet spot for maximum cash flow was 11 p.m. to 9 a.m. on a flow back project. Night after night I drove and loaded and drove and unloaded and drove again, round and round in a loop that covered about fifty miles, mostly over that horrible Road 12.

Once I learned the system, I also had to acknowledge a few realities of my own body including the need for at least a few hours of sleep each night. Many of the drivers around me managed to run continuously for days with no sleep at all as they chased the money. My body demanded that I sleep each night for at least three hours starting around midnight and I found ways to comply. Three hours of sleep each night combined with a half hour nap in the afternoon was enough to get me through most assignments. Awakened by an alarm on my cell phone each day at 3 a.m., I would brew a pot of coffee and rejoin the race to maximum income.

Fuel for the truck was the other undeniable need and that could only be met with a trip back to town. After fueling the truck I would tackle the basics of food and hygiene. I found a laundromat that also had showers much cleaner than the one at the shop. The clothes I had with me translated into two loads of laundry. Washed and dried at the laundromat, they did not smell of diesel fuel and while the laundry was spinning through its cycles, I could buy a hot shower in a clean bathroom. The shower was a metered setup dispensing one minute of fresh water for each dollar token I dropped in to the slot. Five dollars was all I could afford but five minutes of hot clean water was a blessing and then I had the full bathroom long enough to shave and put on clean clothes which always helped my mood. The next stop would be the grocery store to restock the truck refrigerator then a few minutes at the company office to drop paperwork. On the afternoon of the first day of my second month in the Bakken, I was clean, fueled, restocked and headed east toward the reservation to wait for an assignment

Before I left the main highway for another four of five days of no frills truck camping, I stopped at a disposal for my last chance this week to use an actual restroom and to see what they had for free food. Sometimes this disposal would have a pot of chili simmering in a crock pot to entice drivers to bring their loads here. Inside the office I found one of our drivers slumped on a couch. John looked like he had been through the wringer. His bloodshot eyes surrounded by dark circles told me he had been up for more than a few days. Assuming I had pulled in with a load of waste, he asked where I was hauling from. "No assignment," I told him. "I am heading out to the top of road thirteen to wait for a dispatch call." John told me he had been hauling production water for eight days from the Independence pad at the end of Road 13. This was a big pad with five operating wells that had been put in service a few weeks ago. Too far out to be tied to a pipeline, the constant flow of oil and wastewater generated by five new wells had to be removed by trucks in a constant, twenty-four hour a day operation. John was working alongside a driver from another company hauling as many loads as he could move. The work had earned him a small fortune but he was getting barely two hours sleep each night. He had made one fast run to town for fuel and food mid-week and then rushed back out for the next load. The dispatcher had apparently forgotten John was out here and left him alone.

Eight days of steady income had been great but now he desperately needed a trip into town for food, laundry and sleep. He was willing to hand this assignment off to me.

After thanking John for giving me his gold mine, I dished up a bowl of hot chili, grabbed a cup of bad coffee and headed for the truck. I had not been that far out on Road 13 but the well sites were usually well marked and John's directions were clear. I found the Independence pad in the dark and pulled in just as the other company's driver pulled away. From the log books inside the pump house I wrote down a few production numbers and, while the vacuum pump moved hot salt water from the storage tanks into my truck, I mentally calculated how fast these wells were producing water and how that would dictate my rounds to and from the disposal.

This water is called production water because it came from a producing well and it is very different from the foul water that came out of a flow-back. This natural salt water rises from the earth along with the crude oil and natural gas coming up the well. The maze of pipes and equipment at the well head separated the water and oil into different tanks while the gas was vented and burned off. In a future day this production water would be carried away in pipelines but for now moving the water off site faster than the well could fill the tanks was a challenge that created a flow of money for drivers.

The waste water from the Independence pad was contracted to a disposal facility I had not been to. The load was heavy forcing me to hold my speed down around the curves and over the steep hills of road thirteen. A short stretch of paved road connected me back to the fourteen miles of potholes we called Road 12. At the stop sign where Road 12 joined the main highway I turned left, taking me in a new direction across a large river in a county I had not seen.

Exile: A Modern Wilderness Journey

This disposal was better than any I had been hauling to. The unloading pad was concrete, not the mud and rock I had seen thus far. They didn't have a bathroom or shower like Steve enjoyed out west, but they had a good selection of food in a warm driver's lounge with windows looking out at the unloading pad. The windows made it possible to wait inside, out of the wind, while large pumps pulled the saltwater off the trucks and into holding tanks. When the truck was empty and the hoses put away, I carried my paperwork back inside to the desk. The attendant had stepped outside for a smoke. In his absence I grabbed a few extra packages of crumb doughnuts, a shrink wrapped sandwich and two cans of soda. Everything about this job was looking great.

Throughout that day and into the next night I made the tedious round trips from well to disposal and back again. The same four albums played over and over from my smartphone through the truck stereo. At midnight on the second day I had been hauling for thirty hours and had built up a small reserve of empty tank space which meant I was moving slightly more water per day than the well was producing. I could afford to sleep, a little, without fear of the tanks overflowing. The rumble of the diesel engine cradled me in a deep sleep for almost three hours. Daylight was still a few hours away when music and a flashing light from the cell phone alarm broke into my dreamless sleep. Moving quickly, I pulled on jeans and a T-shirt before moving the truck from the corner of the pad where I was sleeping and over to the loading platform. I hoped three hours had not been too long and the tanks would still be at safe levels. Pulling on the heavy parka, I climbed out of the truck and stared in awe at the stars in a moonless sky. I was many miles from any lights and the view was stunning. After connecting the hose and opening the valves, I huddled behind the downwind side of the truck where I could feel a little heat from the hot salt water filling the tank.

Just before sunrise broke over the horizon that morning I was unloading at the disposal and shared a few minutes of small talk with a driver from another company. He seemed like a nice guy, from somewhere in the upper Midwest. Near Chicago, I think he said. We compared notes about assignments, how our respective companies treated us and how both of our dispatchers seemed to be clueless. Transferring our water to the disposal took about twenty minutes. We finished at almost the same time, loaded hoses back on the tankers and climbed into separate trucks. I never asked his name, or maybe I did and just immediately forgot. It wasn't important, we weren't out to here make friends. He gave a short blast on his air horn and waved as he pulled away first.

Driving around the back of the disposal lot toward the highway I had a deep sense that I knew this guy. Had I worked with him on some job in the past? Had he been a firefighter with me thirty years ago in northern Colorado? No, I would remember that. The sun rising over the horizon illuminated the hills around me as I accelerated the empty truck onto the highway turning west toward the well. At the crest of a long and steep downhill grade I downshifted twice and switched on the engine brake to hold back my descent.

I was still pondering the encounter at the disposal as I drove back to the well. That stranger felt so familiar, like I had to have known him from somewhere. The internal voice I was learning to recognize spoke up to say, 'He's your Guardian Angel". "Hmm, that's cool," I thought to myself (or was I answering God?). Over the course of the day the whole issue disappeared from my brain as I continued my trips around the sixty-mile repetitive loop from well to disposal and back again.

Saturday morning broke the same as most mornings on the winter plains of the Dakotas. The sky was cold and gray above a brown winter landscape with a cold wind blowing through everything. The road, as always, was rough and frozen and long and tedious and boring. This truck had ten gears and I needed every one of them to move these heavy loads up and down the hills. The trip to the disposal started with a gradual two mile climb from the shore of the lake up a slowly winding road to the crest of a ridgeline. After crossing a cattle guard at the top, the road meandered along the ridge for half a mile and then plunged hard down into a ravine. The creek bed in the bottom of the ravine was dry in winter and I could see wildlife trails winding through the leafless willow trees that lined the creek bed. A steel culvert waited to carry spring rain under the road which turned to the left and started a steep ascent up the other side of the ravine.

Maintaining momentum was critical for climbing these steep hills with a heavy load. Any mistake in the process of shifting through the ten gears would kill that momentum and result in some degree of disaster. The only way to correct a missed shift was to come to a complete stop and start the whole process again from low gear. Very few trucks have enough low end torque to pull away from a full stop with this much weight on a hill this steep and mine was not one of them. Missing a gear shift on the uphill usually means a driver would have to back down the steep slope to the bottom of the ravine and start again in low gear. Maneuvering a heavily loaded truck backwards down a steep hill could easily have ended with the truck in either a ditch or the creek bed, possibly upside down.

I had no delusions about my driving skill and I chose to rely on a method for hills that was slow and steady with minimal risk. Sixth gear together with the engine brake was a safe way to limit my speed on the downhill. A light touch on the airbrakes was needed to help the engine brake restrain the whole rig but I had to be very light. Too much pressure held for too long would overheat the brakes and if they overheated they would fail. Slowing slightly in the bottom of the ravine I downshifted to fourth gear, which I knew was the right power range to carry the weight of this rig up the other side of the ravine with no more shifting.

The uphill was just over a half a mile long followed by a stretch of flat land. Climbing slowly in fourth gear was a certain method to get to the top without shifting. My biggest risk was that some speed freak behind me would not recognize what I was doing, fly down the hill and catch me crawling up the other side. This was not a place for two trucks to pass. Fortunately, the Independence pad was way off the beaten path. I hadn't seen another truck this far out all morning, but I had checked the mirrors at the top of the ridgeline just to be sure I was alone. With most of the climb behind, the top of the hill was just starting to round off ahead of me and was not as steep approaching the crest.

Less than a hundred yards from the top of the hill a horrible sound like a collision of steel on steel exploded from under the truck. The floorboard shook under my feet and I heard the hissing of broken air hoses. Years of experience immediately told me the driveshaft had torn loose leaving me with no way to continue moving forward. The driveshaft was the connection that delivered power from the engine to the rear wheels to push the rig forward and over the top of the hill. The hissing sound of rushing air told me the severed drive shaft had shredded plastic air lines under the truck. I had only a few minutes before the reserve air stored in tanks would be lost. Without the air from those tanks the brakes would lock into parking mode, leaving me stranded in a precarious position on this steep hillside. The heavy load of saltwater on a hill this steep was probably more than the parking brakes can hold. In a few minutes, or less, I would find myself rolling slowly backward towards the bottom of the ravine unable to stop. Once that started, I would have to decide to either ride the uncontrollable truck backwards to the creek, or jump from the cab and allow the truck to crash at the bottom without me. If this had happened at the bottom of the hill I probably could have rolled backwards to the flat spot over the creek. But I was almost a half mile up the hill which was too much distance to try and steer in reverse with no brakes. Even if the brakes hold a little, enough for a slow descent, I had a high probability of ending in one of the ditches on either side of the road with the whole rig upside down and me inside. The whole scenario raced through my mind in an instant as I scanned the side of the road for a large rock. I was trying to decide if I could set the parking brake, jump out and grab a rock and get it under a tire to hold the truck or would the whole thing start rolling before I could get the rock under the wheel? The human mind can process incredible amounts of information in a very short time when it has to.

Immediately to my left a driveway connected to a well pad. The pad stood out in my mind because it was still under construction and was not yet producing. During the week the site had been full of construction workers assembling the mass of equipment needed to manage a well. This dreary Saturday the construction team decided to stay home. As I scanned the road looking for the perfect rock to block my wheels, I saw another tanker pulling out of the unfinished well pad. I didn't have time to wonder why he was coming from an inoperative well. The other truck pulled left out of the driveway then angled sharply to the right stopping barely ten feet in front of my disabled rig. The driver jumped out of his cab, grabbed a chain from the storage racks along the side of his tank and sprinted to the front of my truck. Without a word, he snapped the chain into the tow hooks of my front bumper and then quickly looped the other end around the back of his tanker. Still holding my foot on the brakes I watched in awe as I realized this was the man I had chatted with two nights ago at the disposal. The man who seemed so familiar I thought I had known him in a previous life. The same man God had said was my guardian angel.

He sprinted back to his cab, scrambled up the steps to the driver's seat and quickly found low gear. I saw the chain go taut between our trucks as his big diesel engine powered into the load of two trucks, mine full of saltwater. I released my foot from the brake pedal. His truck was jumping and bucking as the tires tried to find enough traction on the dirt road to get us both moving up the final one hundred yards of hill. His spinning wheels threw dirt and rocks as black smoke bellowed out both exhaust stacks. I felt my truck begin to roll, just barely, forward, not back to the ravine. An almost silent cheer slipped from my mouth as we moved slowly towards the crest of the hill and then on to flat land. The truck in front of me angled to the side of the road dragging me out of the main traffic path. Sitting now on flat land, I pulled my yellow parking brake control and shut off the engine then jumped from the cab to find several large rocks to block my truck tires. When he could see my wheels were blocked in, the truck in front backed up a few feet releasing tension on the tow chain. I unhooked the chain between the trucks and exhaled a giant sigh knowing this chain and that truck had just saved me from an experience that could have been so much worse.

The other driver climbed out of his cab and walked slowly to the rear of his truck. I was speechless for a minute, trying to calm down from the adrenaline rush of the past two minutes. He asked if I was okay and did I have a phone? After assuring him I could reach help and that I had food and warmth for the wait, I handed over his tow chain. Returning to his cab, he drove away. Over the next week I passed this man several times always going opposite directions. We did not cross paths again at the disposal and we never spoke.

Even though my life had been lived mostly within the church, I could not say that I honestly believed the idea of miracles and divine interventions in our modern times. I understood many people claimed miraculous things were happening in their life but I was confident there was a practical explanation behind each event. The miraculous cure of cancer could be explained by the skill of the doctor, etc. Now I was forced to change my belief. God introducing this driver as my guardian angel followed by his presence and help at that precise moment was too specific. I understood that skeptics could write this off as a coincidence, that the driver was simply in the right place at the right time, but I could not explain it away that casually. I knew in my soul that God had deliberately protected me from harm. This was too clear, too direct and too personal to deny. My prayers of the previous year seeking to fully know God were being answered in tangible situations more real than I had ever known.

The process known as "fracking a well" used enormous volumes of fresh water, mixed with chemicals, and pushed down the well under extreme pressure to open up cracks in the rock more than a mile below the earth's surface. Exactly what was mixed with the water was a mystery to me but I discovered that coming back out of the well the water was hot, oily, smelled bad and had clumps of strange looking crud that often plugged up my tank valves. This wastewater coming out of a completed frack had to be trucked to a disposal well where it would be pumped into the earth. Hauling wastewater from a flow-back operation runs twenty four hours a day, nonstop for a week or more until all the water has been moved.

Moving quickly, driving a little fast, pushing hard to unload and get back to reload was the way to maximize the income of a flow-back and all of this had to happen within a window of opportunity which would close in a matter of days. Flow-back and production water were the only two operations I had been a part of but I had heard other drivers talk about hauling fresh water used to start the fracking process.

A giant metal tank, called a Poseidon, would be assembled near a well pad and made water tight with a rubber liner bigger than I could have imagined existed. For a week, sometimes more, prior to the start of fracking, a parade of water haulers would bring fresh water from a nearby well and pump the water into the Poseidon tank. Each tank could hold more than a million gallons of fresh water and it was not unusual to have multiple tanks on a frack site.

Everything about the fresh water operation sounded to me like a hassle. This was winter and the fresh water would freeze causing a variety of mechanical problems. Drivers carried propane torches to thaw out frozen valves and hoses. The loading and unloading process always had leaks and spills which created dangerous ice slicks. Before hauling fresh water a truck's five thousand gallon water tanker had to be cleaned inside and out. The fresh water could not be contaminated by the remains from a prior assignment hauling flow-back. Often the drivers would get their tanks cleaned, and then some problem would delay the operation. They would sit idle, with no income, protecting their clean tank waiting for the fresh water to begin.

My rookie mind was convinced that flow-back and production were the ideal opportunities. While other drivers sat protecting their clean tanks, I was out hauling the nastiest, foulest waste the oil field could puke up. When they were all sitting out of service waiting to haul fresh water, I became the go to guy for waste, answering any call that came up and raking in a solid income. My mood soured quickly on the day the dispatcher told me to clean my tank and get ready for an upcoming fresh water haul. Grudgingly I prepared to join in by opening the hatches on top of my vacuum tank that are large enough for a man to crawl inside. Gazing inside the tank for the first time since starting this job, I was grateful someone else would be climbing inside to pressure wash the interior of the tanker. The next day we left the shop in early afternoon and headed to the fresh water pickup depot as a procession of six trucks. We each took our turn pulling a load of fresh water into the tanker at the water depot before heading to the well pad to push that water into the Poseidon tank. My first load was complete in an hour and I returned to the depot for a second load surprised to find fourteen trucks from other companies lined up at the depot. I went to the end of the line and joined the stop and go procession of trucks who were earning nothing as they waited. For nearly two hours we crawled, stop and go, stop and go, in a line that would sit for a few minutes, and then slowly move up one truck length. When the front truck moved into the loading position, every truck behind would move forward. This was not a reasonable approach produced through good thinking but it was the accepted method. Crawl eighty feet and wait. If you didn't move up you risked losing your place, which meant sleep or a nap or even dinner was not an option. I fumed at the stupidity of this process. There was no one in charge, just a line of drivers from different companies all competing for the income that was paid per load. With this much waiting my rate of income per day was looking terrible.

After delivering my second load I returned to find the same slow crawl and what looked to me like a growing line of trucks. In disgust over the process I decided to go to the shop for repairs on a small air leak I had been ignoring. Maybe I could use the mechanical problem as an excuse to completely bail out of this fresh water assignment and get back to hauling flow-back. Pulling out of the waiting line, I drove the hour and a half back to town. Parked inside the shop a mechanic started on the simple repair, while I vented my frustration to the company owner. Practically begging to be returned to flow-back, I presented my case of why I should be pulled from this money losing activity of fresh water. Stewart, the owner, was an old trucker who had fallen into the right place at the right time. He was just a driver when this Bakken boom started. He partnered with his older brother to buy a couple of trucks, turn some contacts and connections into a contract and this trucking company was launched. In my mind I was confident I had far more business knowledge than this old trucker, but I managed to hold my tongue when he told me to go back to the fresh water haul and be patient.

Patient is not a word my friends would use to describe me. Often impulsive, sometimes impetuous, I had launched businesses by seizing opportunity when it presented. Sitting in line, fighting a crowd for a turn at hauling fresh water was clearly not an opportunity. But, I wasn't the boss here. This was not my call to make. He owned the truck, he called the shots and I needed the job. I headed back to the fresh water haul. My life, especially my finances, didn't give me the option of being belligerent.

Driving back to the fresh water depot God jogged my memory of recent reading and study. Last year when I was devouring our small home library I opened my wife's collection of Beth Moore books and started reading Beth's unique insight to Christian life. Two of the books had come with me to the oil field. It seemed almost comical to be reading a woman's devotional out here in the all-male environment of the oil field but I really enjoyed Beth Moore's style of writing.

I could not say exactly how my various readings, including Beth's words, had molded this together but recently four words had come together through my study. These four simple words, linked together in a statement I did not yet understand, flashed through my mind: Obedience, Perseverance, Patience and Trust. None of those words fit any aspect of my life yet God seemed to be highlighting them as a mantra.

When these words showed up in my mind again as I drove, I realized I was learning how to differentiate God's words from my own mental ramblings. It dawned on me that God usually said things I would have never thought of on my own. Truly, God's words are not man's words. These four words were something that my rebellious and prideful spirit had not strung together in more than three decades of adult life. No one who knew me would expect me to claim these four words as a mantra. This could only be God.

Night was falling when I pulled into the fresh water depot. I found my place at the end of a line of trucks waiting to load. The stop and go crawl along the shoulder of the road was clearly shorter and moving faster. There was more of a rhythm to the process than I had seen in the afternoon. My tanker was full in less than a half hour and as I drove to the well pad I could see the trucks had spread out over the eight-mile haul route. The original crowd of tankers was now scattered out driving the eight-mile route, or working at the loading and unloading points. The lines of trucks at each end were almost gone. Under the lights of portable power plants and truck mounted flood lights I connected to the curved pipe we called a candy cane that would carry my water up twenty feet to the rim of the giant tank. My five thousand gallons made no noticeable change to the water level inside the tank but I enjoyed climbing the portable stairs that gave us a vantage point to watch the progress. When my tank was empty I stowed my hoses and started another trip to the depot. By the time I returned an hour later there were only two trucks waiting in line. That pace remained steady throughout the night.

Eight miles was a short haul and none of it was on Road 12. Fresh water weighed less than flow-back which meant larger loads were easier to haul at higher speeds. The night turned into a fresh water gold mine as I calculated in my head how much I was earning on each load. Of course Stewart had known this would happen when he sent me back out. He wasn't fooled by the slow start up. If I had won my argument with him I would have missed out on what I now understood was a great source of oil field income. Unaware at the moment how long this lesson was going to continue, I began to unravel the meaning of Obedience, Perseverance, Patience and Trust.

The dispatcher who controlled our assignments had never driven a truck, never worked in the oil field and never run a business. He was a carpenter who decided to try something different. Stewart was in need of a dispatcher and help was hard to find in this boom town. The local taco shop was paying twenty dollars an hour to staff the drive up window. Stewart would have taken any warm body able to operate a cell phone to fill this role and thus the dispatcher was hired. We all knew he didn't have a clue what he was doing.

With my business background I may have been quicker than some to do the math on the earning potential of different projects. Certain assignments had better income than others and I was here for maximum income. I watched the dispatcher pull drivers from high paying fresh water assignments to send them out on dirty, low paying service work that was not urgent and could have been held. He didn't understand prioritizing the work to get the best return for either the drivers or the company. Instead of truly dispatching, this misplaced carpenter responded to incoming phone calls in any manner that moved the service request off his desk as quickly as possible.

The dispatcher's decisions would affect, for good or bad, the drivers' incomes. My turn to feel the effect came on a warm day in late March as I was pushing my fifth payload of the day into a Poseidon tank. This was a fresh water assignment in good weather with a short haul and only a dozen trucks. We were all running in a good rhythm producing steady income and spirits were high. When the phone rang I saw the dispatcher's phone number on the screen and considered not answering. On the third ring, with a tone of dread in my voice, I accepted the call. Just as I feared, he was pulling me off the fresh water money maker to go handle a service call at a remote well. Nothing about this felt good and I really wanted to argue my way out of the assignment. For reasons I couldn't explain, I held my tongue, wrote down the instructions and ended the phone call. I didn't realize the mantra was at work. I was about to understand the meaning and value of Obedience.

The drive to the service call took almost an hour over the usual rough roads through the hills of the Bakken. The trip brought me to a new part of the reservation I had not seen. I found the well foreman and asked what he needed. A valve on a pump had failed, allowing waste water from the well to spill across the nearly level five acre well pad. The gravel pad was now contaminated with a thin layer of waste water that needed to be sucked up by a vacuum truck, and I was driving a vacuum truck.

The work was paid by the hour, not by the load and would be both physically demanding and incredibly boring. Stretching out and connecting together every rubber hose I had, I began the tedious chore of sucking up the thin pool of waste water spread over and through the gravel lot. This was going to be an all afternoon task dragging heavy hoses surrounded by the noise of the truck engine and the screaming vacuum pump. There was nothing fun about this including working for the lowest pay level a water hauler must endure. Every part of me wanted to make up an excuse to bail out and go back where the money was, but I had nothing. If I faked a mechanical problem I would have to go the shop, not back to fresh water and being at the shop paid nothing. No good excuse or argument came to mind so I stayed and methodically sucked water from the gravel lot. My foul mood prevented me from seeing what was really happening. Following in the footsteps of Obedience, Perseverance was now in play.

Six hours later as the sun was setting, I loaded and secured my hoses, filled out the service call paperwork and headed for the disposal. What should have been a six payload afternoon had been reduced to an hourly wage and a long drive to dump the water miles away from the normal disposals. This type of water, sucked up from a parking lot rather than directly out of a well, could not be taken to most disposals. This water would only be accepted at a few designated sites which meant I was headed miles in the wrong direction from where the fresh water had been paying good money.

After unloading at the special disposal well I was too close to town to not get fuel. I joined the line of headlights headed west and tried to count how many gas flares I could see on the hillsides, until the lights of town came into view. My mind was feeling the day had been a waste as I filled the fuel tanks, stopped at the market for groceries and went to the shop to drop off paperwork.

Rounding the corner from street to shop I was surprised to see every truck this company owned lined up in the yard. This many parked trucks meant neither the company nor the drivers were making money. Something had caused the field operations to halt, at least temporarily. Inside the shop, I asked what happened to the fresh water haul. The mechanics told me a pump had broken at the water depot which ended the high money operation I had been pulled from. Barely fifteen minutes after I left, every truck was sent away. On the other side of the reservation, sucking up that parking lot spill, I had been the only truck with work all afternoon. Instead of sitting back at the yard with the others, that service call made me the only driver earning income for the second half of the day.

Several more lessons had to happen before the entire concept clicked in my brain. Similar situations unfolded over the next weeks but I responded differently each time. The next lesson started immediately following a noon lunch of cold chicken and stale biscuits from the grocery store deli that had been bouncing around in my truck mini refrigerator for three days. I was pushing fresh water into a Poseidon tank on the top of a hill with a beautiful view of the rolling countryside and a lake below. Eight trucks were parked side-by-side with hoses connecting each truck to a huge pipe that stretched one hundred feet across the parking area and up the side of the Poseidon. The combined pump pressure of eight big diesel engines lifted the water twenty feet to the open top of the tank where it sprayed out in a giant stream before splashing to the water surface which was slowly rising inside the tank. The noise of the engines and the pumps made conversation impossible. A thin layer of melting snow covering the frozen ground transformed dragging hoses into a dangerous physical task. While waiting for their tanks to empty, some drivers would smoke a cigarette. Others might eat a snack or make use of the cold and smelly portable toilets. I used the twenty minutes of unloading time as a lunch break, eating my meal while sitting in the driver's seat until a change in the pitch of the pump noise told me my tank was empty. Climbing down from the cab, I flung the chicken bones into the prairie for the coyotes to find, stowed away the heavy rubber hose and tried to kick some slush off my boots before climbing back into the driver's seat. The drive tires spun on the ice as I pulled my now empty truck away from the discharge pipe, opening up an empty slot to be filled by a loaded truck from the staging area.

Before I could get off the well pad, my phone rang and the dispatcher's number appeared on the smartphone screen. I felt that instant dread of knowing he would have something ridiculous to say that would probably cost me money. Not hearing from the dispatcher, sometimes for days, was best and I was really hoping to stay with this high paying assignment for at least another two days.

Just as I feared, he wanted me to leave this fresh water haul to go handle a service call. I knew the call was not a priority and it would pay both me and the company less than half of what I was earning here. He just wanted the customer request off his desk and I had lost the lottery. As he described the specifics of the task he tossed out a slang name for a special tool that was needed for this job. A filter, placed inside the suction hose, to prevent rocks from being sucked into the load. The cone-shaped steel filter was called a "witches hat." I knew what it was and I had one with me and yet without a conscious thought, I immediately played on my rookie status in a ploy to avoid this assignment. "Witches Hat," I asked? "What's that? Are you saying I have to wear a special hat for this job?" The dispatcher fell for the ruse, apparently too busy with his own life to even explain what I pretended not to know. In a moderately disgusted tone he simply said never mind and hung up.

Exile: A Modern Wilderness Journey

I was smiling over my cleverness as I turned out of the well pad. With a quick tap on the foot peddle I checked the brakes and pushed the gearshift lever into fourth gear to slow my descent down the steep, half mile hill in front of me. At the bottom of the hill the narrow dirt track flattened out before connecting to a two lane gravel road that was surprisingly dry and in good condition. Proud of my quick thinking and chuckling to myself about deflecting that service call, I crossed the cattle guard and accelerated toward the fresh water loading site. I reached for the earbuds that hung on the dash next to the phone. Steve would enjoy hearing this story and could share in my delight. We all appreciated an opportunity to outwit the dispatcher and we loved to share these stories. Before I could press the speed dial for Steve's phone number, my thoughts were crushed by a loud single pop followed by an ominous hiss from under the truck. A quick turn into the next well pad was followed by a buzzing alarm from the dashboard. The gauges showed air pressure declining rapidly. Another minute and this truck would be immobilized because loss of air means locked brakes. Wherever I could get to before that gauge dove below fifty was going to be the end of my day. I was grateful to make it off the main road, away from the noise of other trucks and the eyes of the other drivers. I shut off the key, killing the engine and silencing the alarm. The sound of air hissing from under the truck continued as I climbed out to investigate.

From the sound of the air leak I could tell this was substantial. Sometimes a small air leak could be ignored for a day or two but this was loud enough I would have to crawl under the truck and lay in the melting snow to look further. My coveralls were going to be completely trashed but there was no other way to determine the extent of this problem. It did not take long to find the broken brass fitting on a primary air tank. Neither ingenuity nor duct tape would solve this, I needed a mechanic which meant a phone call to the dispatcher followed by a long wait to be rescued. My great money making day had just become a no income waste of time. Immobilized, waiting for a mechanic to repair the truck, I tried to find something to read and not watch the other trucks moving back and forth making money while I made nothing.

In usual fashion, the mechanic arrived more than four hours later. Phone calls and texted photos had conveyed to him the problem, so at least he could have the correct part with him. A part he had to scrounge the town's supply houses to find. When the mechanic crawled out from under the truck and started loading his tools the sun was setting and the air temperature was falling fast. This was going to be a cold night that would freeze everything from the ruts in the road to the valves on the truck. A beautiful day had turned into a miserable night.

This cycle repeated over the next two weeks until my brain finally spotted the pattern. My Obedience and Perseverance, or lack thereof, was directly affecting both my income and my lifestyle. God was trying to teach me to let Him call the shots. The lesson to grasp was that I was here to take orders, which was a new concept for this former business owner accustomed to running the show. God wanted me to give up control and be willing to go anywhere. In addition to learning the mantra, these very clear, very specific lessons were developing my understanding that exile is not punishment. Exile was unfolding as a training ground. This first step of the training in the harsh conditions of the oil field was similar to military boot camp. The isolation provided freedom from distractions and my lack of options for creating income held me here through the toughest lessons.

My eyes and my heart were open and aware. I became conscious of teachable moments. The discomfort and misery made the lessons more intense which I would later understand translated into a longer lasting education.

When I grasped the full realization of the first two parts of the mantra, Obedience and Perseverance, God then assured me that Patience on my part and a Trust in His plan would complete the mantra. He was not, however, offering any statements about how long this would take.

Just as this first set of lessons became clear, I went home for a short break. I had been mostly alone, working day and night in harsh winter conditions for five weeks and I was just beginning to realize my understanding of "faith in God" was being rewritten. He was taking me deeper into Christianity than I had ever allowed myself to go. These experiences were too real to deny and yet if I knew if I ever shared these many people would rationalize the events away as coincidences wrapped up in emotions. If these stories were ever revealed, most people, even many claiming to be Christian, would slide me across the pew to the crazy category.

My break at home was no more than a long weekend where I did little besides sleep. I enjoyed the company of my wife but I had little to give back to her as I was physically and emotionally exhausted. My dream of a life in Belize was on hold, if not dead. The big residential project that promised me a job had now gone more than a year without funding. Construction on my Belize house was stalled while I tried to grind out a living in the oil field. The friends with the guest house were flexible and Belize was entering the non-tourist season so my clothes could remain in their house but I could not afford to go use them.

The break ended too soon and I joined another flight of quiet men in coveralls jammed into a tiny regional jet headed back to the Bakken. The two-hour flight was time for my mind to retrace how life had changed. Before this oil field gig I had not held a typical job or reported to a boss in almost fourteen years. Ten of those years had raced by when I was the owner of a growing business, followed by a long sabbatical in Belize. When life forced me to put the Belize house on hold and head home in search of income I looked on the Internet for a conventional job that would pay our bills. The Belize resort project was my goal, but I needed a means of survival while I waited for that to materialize. To fund this interim period, I applied for jobs on line. Dozens and dozens of resumes and job applications had gone out and the only result was my learning the modern system of online hiring had no interest in my experience or skill set. Dozens of resume submittals attracted the interest of exactly no one. Starting another business was out of the question since I had no idea for a business and no capital for start-up.

Stuffed into the small seats of a regional jet with a cabin full of oil field workers, I tried to imagine a long term life as a water hauler since that appeared to be my only choice. Could I accept the idea that this might go on longer than I wanted it to? Oil prices were still rising and everyone thought the Bakken had another twenty years of drilling ahead. Maybe I could find a way to make a life out of this.

Exile: A Modern Wilderness Journey

Returning to North Dakota on this mid-day flight, I landed at a small town an hour's drive south of the shop. Steve was busy and the only pickup I could arrange from the airport was with the dispatcher. The mechanics needed parts from a dealer in this town so the dispatcher was willing to deliver both the parts and me back to the shop. He drove like a crazed demon in his company provided pickup truck. I tried to make small talk and hoped he didn't kill me while he passed on hills; chain smoked and answered cell phone calls. When we arrived at the truck yard, I thanked him for the ride, grabbed my suitcase and climbed into my big blue Freightliner. Settling in was easier this time. I fueled the truck, bought groceries and returned to the shop hoping for a good night's sleep before I would grudgingly return to the oil field tomorrow.

Those plans were ruined when my phone rang and the screen showed the dispatcher's number. I was parked barely fifty feet from the office, I could see him standing in the window looking at my truck and I understood why he wouldn't walk in the wind to come pound on my door. The dispatcher told me to drop the vacuum tanker and hook up to a flatbed trailer then come into the shop for a box of tie-down straps. Thirty minutes later, with the flatbed connected to my tractor, I parked in the northwest corner of the yard and watched as one of the yard hands forklifted a load of giant white plastic bags onto the flatbed. He helped me strap down the twenty-two bags and explained that each bag held two thousand pounds of a wood fiber used at drilling rigs to absorb waste fluids coming out of the drill operation. It was now 8 p.m. on a Sunday and I knew the weather forecast was calling for substantial amounts of wind driven snowfall.

The dispatcher gave me instructions on how to find the well and I headed to the two lane highway as darkness settled in and the snow began to fall. In the course of five miles, the snow changed from nothing to light to heavy as it swirled across the road in the increasing wind. Thirty minutes into the trip visibility had dropped to a quarter mile with snow blowing horizontal across the roadway. My truck was at full legal weight on a two lane road winding through hill country in the dark in a snow storm. I asked myself, "In what alternate universe would this make sense?" A rational person would cancel this trip until the snow blew away, probably tomorrow morning. Finding a spot to sleep would have been the intelligent choice but my time here had impressed on me the lesson that oil field operations obey neither rational thought nor intelligent choice.

The small green posts with reflectors shining in my headlights were the only way to identify the roadway as the blowing snow became a whiteout. Traffic had thinned to something I had not seen in this normally bustling boom country. Apparently, this storm was bad enough that even oil field people found a reason to get off the road. Everything within me wanted to quit. To pull off in a safe spot, call the dispatcher, and refuse to proceed. But one voice was telling me to push on. Quitting would create problems with the company. This load needed to be delivered or they would not have sent me out. I felt a reassurance to just drive slow and careful and trust that things would be okay. That quiet voice was telling me I was capable of more than I realized if I would give up control and just trust God.

In my life, I have started businesses from nothing, built multi-million dollar projects, managed employees and negotiated the many challenges of owning a business. In my youth, I was a firefighter and EMT working inside burning buildings and rescuing people from all types of accidents and disasters. I have not been hidden from challenge or difficulty. But this oil field experience was something different on a gut level. The constant harsh demands of this lifestyle were shredding my established logic. The challenges out here forced me to override sensible thinking. With no other option to fall back on, I was discovering a new level of commitment to accomplishing life. What appeared impossible was becoming routine. Driving through this North Dakota blizzard gave me a new sense that, in partnership with God, I could tackle any challenge. The tangible challenges of daily life in the Bakken were giving me a slowly unfolding realization of what can be accomplished when I trust God beyond my ability to understand. He was teaching me a trust that didn't just override fear, it eliminated fear entirely. God was showing me what absolute trust looks like and to apply it to everyday tasks. He was teaching me that trust is not relevant to the trial or the task. Rather, trust is relevant only to His grace, His power and His authority over everything.

My route through the storm was a road I had covered more times in the past few weeks than I could remember. What few landmarks I could see were familiar including the intersection with Road 12. On this trip, I would not have to cover the entire fourteen miles. My turn off was barely two miles beyond the highway where I found a single track reservation road I had not yet been on. Darkness and blowing snow concealed everything except the dirt trail within a hundred feet of my bumper where the low beam headlights cut through the blowing snow. Ironically, the wind was blowing so hard the snow would not stick to the frozen road. My destination was well marked and after only a few winding miles I could see the lights of the drill tower in the snowy sky. Under normal conditions this drive would have taken an hour and half. Tonight I had been driving through this storm for slightly more than three hours.

Randall L. Cumley

Unloading in the blizzard at midnight, I asked the forklift operator if this trip was really necessary. He explained that the drill rig would have had to shut down if I had not delivered. Shutting down an active drill rig creates expensive problems. Delivering this load really had been critical.

Safety regulations on the well sites prohibited drivers sleeping in trucks on site. My only choice was to drive back out into the blizzard on the narrow dirt road in search of a safe place to park for the night. By 2 a.m. I was back on Road 12, where I found a wide spot to pull off and make my camp. With the diesel engine running for heat, the rumble and vibration was soothing and I slept deeply a full eight hours until the sound of tire chains broke into my sleep. The rattle and ring of steel chains going round and round on the wheels of moving trucks is a distinctive sound. As much as I wanted to remain in the warmth of my bunk forever, I had to look outside. This was a primary route through the oil field which was heavily traveled and well worn. Tire chains were usually needed only for the small side roads accessing the well pads. By the time a truck made it out to Road 12 the chains were usually removed. The sound of tire chains interrupting my sleep was not normal.

Pulling back the blackout curtains on the passenger window, I could see Road 12 was a sheet of ice polished by the wind and surrounded by drifts of snow. While I had been asleep a half dozen trucks had pulled in around me on this wide shoulder of the road, barely out of the lane of traffic. The normal flow of trucks that had ceased in last night's blizzard had now resumed. Road conditions were abysmal but trucks were moving. The slowly clearing sky would soon allow sunshine to melt the ice that covered every road. I had no pending assignment and no desire to join the slow parade of chained up trucks grinding slowly over the winding hills on slippery roads. I dropped the curtain, switched off my phone ringer and crawled back into the bunk.

Slightly after noon I pulled open the curtains that covered the front windows and snapped them into their stowed position. The sun was shining in a clear blue sky and the wind, oddly, was not blowing. Patches of dirt were beginning to show through the ice that covered the only road in and out of the reservation. It would be at least two more hours before the warmth of the sun could combine with the truck traffic to churn this glare ice back into the slush covered skating rink that was inevitable this time of year. My truck was stocked with food, plenty of books, good music and a warm bunk. I was in no hurry to rejoin the carnival but instead decided to accept this day as a financial loss, choosing instead to dig in to my study.

Searching different sources on my own did not seem to be bringing together any specific answers for the questions I had raised in Belize but I was learning a lot of new thoughts on a variety of topics. What I did not yet realize is that my reading was gathering together pieces of a large puzzle. Looking back later I would realize God was willing to answer my initial questions of a year ago but I lacked a foundation to be able to understand His answer. He was guiding me through a process of collecting the pieces that would soon be assembled to create that foundational understanding. While He built my understanding, God was also physically, tangibly demonstrating His involvement in very specific details of my life. An individualized involvement that would lead me to the answers I had asked for.

This was only going to work if I could be patient enough to remain obedient and persevere through the training process. I would have to trust God to put this all together. Again, He was showing me the mantra of Obedience, Perseverance, Patience and Trust.

The weeks slipped by in a repetitive pattern with little variation. I took another short break at home, not nearly long enough. Scanning the online employment ads revealed no new opportunities. Paying the bills required I return, grudgingly, to the oil field. The weather was trying to warm up which brought a new set of problems. It was spring in North Dakota, also known as the mud season. Storms would pop up quickly covering the roads with several inches of wet, heavy snow. When the clouds moved out the sun would turn the moisture into impassable roads. The frozen ruts of winter were now vehicular Slip N' Slides traversed by trucks covered from tire to exhaust stack with layers of mud. Working at the well pads, pulling hoses through the mud, increased the physical demands of the job. Driving required tire chains be put on for the mud roads and taken off for paved roads. Installing or removing tire chains on a semi is an annoyance in the winter that becomes a misery in the mud. Clothing and gloves become coated in slimy mud which would get tracked into the cab and transferred to everything inside. Outside, the mud covered over headlights and obscured valves and controls. Driving was no longer a skill, it became an art form. One veteran driver commented we were not actually controlling the trucks but were merely along for the ride. Our efforts to steer or stop, he says, are nothing more than suggestions that the truck move in a desired direction. Gravity and mud would ultimately determine where the truck would wind up, and often that combination led to the ditch.

One night, one of our young drivers slid off a muddy curve and became hopelessly stuck in the shallow ditch adjacent to the main road. He called the dispatcher to let the office know he wouldn't be hauling any water the rest of the night and would need a tow to get out. No one was going to rescue him until the next day so he got as comfortable as he could in a truck that was leaning slightly to one side. He had barely spread out inside his bunk for some needed sleep when his truck was slammed broadside by another truck sliding off the same muddy curve. The other truck ricocheted off Phil's like an old-time pinball game bouncing right back onto the road and continuing on. Picking himself off the floor where the collision had thrown him, the driver took a few minutes to regain his nerves before returning to the bunk. Before he could fall asleep another truck slid off the road and ricocheted off Phil's tilting truck/home just like the first, bouncing back to the road and continuing on. Phil realized sleep was not an option and he decided to just stay up sitting in the seat furthest from the road. He was hit two more times before a winch truck pulled him out the next day. When he got back to the shop he moved his personal belongings to his car and drove away, ending his oil field job without so much as a goodbye.

8

Just before 9 p.m., at the end of another long day, I was finished fighting the mud. Pulling onto the familiar stretch of highway that ran alongside the reservation, I turned toward town and sighed slightly, happy to be on dry pavement. In the weeks of camping every night I had assembled in my mind an inventory of places for overnight parking. Ahead on the right was a short service road leading to a quiet well pad that was a good spot to camp outside the reservation. I had learned there were three distinct areas of operation in this part of the Bakken and this camping spot was a good starting point to head towards whatever assignment the dispatcher might call with. Parking behind the pump control building hid me from the lights and noise of the highway and the view to the east would be a great sunrise, if I was still here by morning.

Randall L. Cumley

Warmer spring weather had ended the need to idle the truck all night for warmth. With the truck shut off, I could enjoy the quiet while I turned to the chore of evening housekeeping in my eight-by-ten home and work space. If there was a way to leave the mud outside the cab I hadn't found it. Sitting on the passenger seat to unlace and pry off wet boots contained the worst of the mud in the front corner of the cab. Within the limited space of the passenger seat, I could squirm out of my insulated coveralls and keep most of the mud they carried within the same space as the boots. Once removed, the coveralls would hang from a hook above the passenger side door in a weak attempt to dry out overnight. Pivoting left on the seat, I could maneuver my feet around the gear shift lever to drop wet socks and damp jeans between the seats. With a small whisk broom I kept behind the driver's seat I moved the mud and dirt that had migrated in over the day forward to the space around the driver's foot pedals. Once the rubber floor mats were swept, I unrolled a small rug I had cut to fit between and behind the seats. This soft and colorful rug defined both the time and the space where the truck transformed from work to home.

This had been a typically long and tiring day and my night routine did not take long. Barely fifteen minutes after pulling into this pad, I had the truck converted into a camper and I was ready to enjoy my nightly treat of six tiny crumb covered donuts from a plastic sleeve with a pint of milk. Not a great diet plan, but it was my comfort food before bed. The temptation to turn off the cell phone was strong. We were supposed to be available at all times for whatever job the dispatcher might have and it was normal to get calls at any hour of the day or night. Tonight I just wasn't in the mood to be awakened for some service call that could have waited till morning. I could always claim there was no cell service when I reappeared tomorrow. But, Obedience spoke to my heart and I made sure the ringer was on high as I lay the phone on the nightstand beside the bed. I sent a text to our dispatcher giving him my location for the night. Exhaustion brought sleep quickly which was good because the phone rang sooner than I had hoped. On the first ring, I really considered ignoring the call. Through the second ring, I pondered the possible consequences of ignoring the call. Obedience flashed through my mind again. On the third ring, I grabbed the cell phone and answered the call. I could see on the screen of the phone it was 2:30 a.m.

All of the well pads were computerized and communicated to a central office. The oil companies have their own radio network throughout the Bakken to monitor and control the wells. Any mechanical problem, on any well, is detected and immediately reported. This call from our dispatcher was waking me up to respond to a well that was reporting high levels in the wastewater storage tanks. If the tanks got too full, the computers would shut down the well stopping, the flow of water, and oil, coming up through the well. In the industry they called this shutting in a well and the companies really hated to see this happen because a shut in well was not producing money.

When a well is drilled and set into production it will bring to the surface oil, water and natural gas. All three have to be processed in some way. On some wells the natural gas is collected into pipes and sold into the nation's natural gas grid. Wells that are too far away from a collection pipeline use flares to burn off the natural gas. The oil is the primary revenue product, collected in tanks and either piped or trucked to a facility where it can be sold. That leaves the water to be disposed of. Sometimes the water can be collected into a pipe grid that covers an entire county. The water is carried through the pipes to a disposal well where it is injected back into the earth. Remote wells too far out to be economically connected to a wastewater grid store the water in tanks to be hauled off by trucks.

The well that was in alarm state in the middle of the night had been recently drilled and all the work to connect into the county wide pipe grid was not complete. The tanks had to be constantly emptied by dedicated water haulers who worked around the clock to move the water off-site. This alarm was an indication that something had happened to a driver who should have been removing the water.

I was the closest truck and could get there the quickest. I knew the well as soon as the dispatcher gave me the name. We hauled flow-back from the fracking operation that opened this well just two weeks ago. Standing up from the bed, I reached across the driver's seat to the ignition key.

As I turned the key the big diesel growled to life, and I sat back down on the bed to clear the sleep from my brain. Perseverance pushed me to ignore that strong desire for another hour of sleep. The little rug was soft on bare feet as I reached into the upper cabinet and treated myself with clean, dry socks and a fresh T-shirt. I rolled the little rug back into its storage spot then pulled on my slightly damp denim jeans. This would be day four in this pair of jeans without benefit of laundry. Standing between the seats, I pulled the muddy coveralls on as gently as I could, trying to keep the mud from flaking off into my sleeping area. I moved up to the passenger seat hoping my boots had dried out at least a little in the barely four hours I had been sleeping. They had not.

In less than five minutes after the phone call I was dressed and headed off the well pad to the main highway. Turning north, I worked through all ten gears in quick succession and enjoyed how quickly this much power could accelerate with an empty trailer. The smartphone pushed soft music through the stereo and I settled in for the forty five minute trip to the well. There was a small town with an all-night truck stop half way between here and the well where I could grab coffee and a plastic wrapped muffin.

The Wyzetta #7 well had been drilled at the end of an unusually good dirt road that ran up and down like a roller coaster track over short, steep hills for a full five miles off the main highway. When the road took an abrupt turn to the south on the top of the biggest hill, the well pad was tucked just to the right, below the crest of the hill and barely off of the curve. Another truck, not from our company, was loading water when I pulled in. He told me he ran a regular route in this region hauling water from other wells owned by the same oil company. When the alarm first sounded the oil company called this driver to the site hoping he could move enough water to keep the well operating until I arrived. We chatted briefly until his tank was full. When he pulled out, I recorded the tank level readings from the computer in the pump house then set about the process of connecting hoses from tanks to the truck. Twenty minutes later I pulled away with 4200 gallons of hot, heavy salt water and started the slow trip out to the highway. Production salt water is almost fifty percent heavier than fresh water. I could feel the weight trying to push the truck around, fighting against my engine brake, opposing my attempts to control descent speed on the down hills, then teaming up with gravity to resist my efforts to climb up the next hill. The wastewater disposal, ten miles from the well, was a newer facility with a good, clean shower free to water haulers. They provided a sparse, but warm, driver's lounge with free hotdogs, popcorn and coffee.

The tank alarms had alerted because our company's assigned driver had gone to a nearby town for dinner then fell asleep in his truck. By the time he woke up to his mistake, I had taken his place and settled in to the rhythm of this well. He showed up ten hours too late and I had the joy of telling him the boss was waiting for him in the office on the other side of the county. He would be sucking slime out of sump pits for weeks as atonement for his mistake.

For me, Obedience and Perseverance had paid off. By camping out in the field rather than the shop and by answering the phone when I wanted to sleep I had landed a water hauler's dream assignment. Almost as good as the jobs Steve had fifty miles east. This would be a steady, predictable routine with scheduled sleep hours, no competing for loads, regular hot showers and free hot dogs.

This well, was now my personal gold mine, shared with one other driver on rotating twelve-hour shifts. No driving Road 12, no phone calls with the dispatcher, just a steady routine of twenty mile round trips on good roads to and from a nearly new disposal. When the other driver took his twelve hour shift I would have time to read, sleep and gaze at the scenery. The sunset from the top of the hill that evening was stunning. The other driver preferred working nights and I was looking forward to ten hours of uninterrupted sleep.

Barely seventy-two hours passed before the dispatcher called to crush the best opportunity I had seen in more than three months of misery. I assumed being the hero who saved this well at 3 a.m. would translate into an extended ride on the gravy train. Contrary to my opinion, the dispatcher felt he was obligated to share the wealth. He was calling to tell me a replacement was on the way, I was being pulled back to the shop. Arguing that I had earned this assignment got me nowhere. I was fuming so much when the other driver showed up that I refused to even explain what was happening on this pad. He could figure it out for himself. As I drove in silent disgust back to the shop, I was angry at the dispatcher but I also had to question God. Why did this assignment, which appeared to me to be a reward for being Obedient and Patient, last only three days? This could have been a great three week money maker that I had earned by following the mantra. Why did I get pulled so quickly? God did not reply.

The next day I was cleaning mud out of the truck in the shop parking lot, when a new driver began settling in to an empty truck parked beside mine. Like many of the drivers out here, Ron was in his mid-fifties, tired of the low paying grind back home and had come to the oil field to get rich. For more than five years stories of high paying jobs in the oil boom had been spreading across the nation bringing men like Ron in search of an opportunity they couldn't find at home. He was from Colorado where he had been driving limousines in Aspen. He had no practical experience in a semi but the previous week he completed two weeks at a trucking school where he learned enough to get a Class A commercial driver's license. Ron had invested several thousand dollars at the training school to get his chance at the boom. The school had taught him what he needed to pass the driver's license test which would probably be just enough to get him in trouble out here.

On this early spring day, the boom seemed to have hit an unusual lull and most of the trucks this company owned were sitting in the yard as melting snow transformed the parking lot into ten acres of mud. For some odd reason we were not involved in any fracking operations although the stream of trucks from other companies on the highway did not seem any smaller than usual. Steve continued to ride his seniority on plum assignments out west along with a half dozen senior drivers, including the one who bumped me from the Wyzetta. Sitting in the yard was earning nothing for the rest of us. I connected to the shop Wi-Fi signal and searched the internet for a different job option hoping something would show up to take me home but found nothing.

Through the day of waiting I vacuumed dirt from the inside of the truck and put away my clean, diesel smelling laundry. While I puttered around with housekeeping I thought I heard God say, "You can go home." I wanted that to be Him, not just my own depression. I walked to the office to deliver a stack of paperwork generated by last week's work. As I slogged through the mud, walking back to the truck I heard, again, "you can go home." I was trying really hard to practice Obedience, Perseverance, Patience and Trust and I didn't recognize these words as anything other than my own wishful thinking.

The second day of sitting in the yard dawned warm and sunny. The drivers were milling around the shop doors enjoying a chance to get out of their trucks on a long-awaited spring day. I wandered slowly up to the group to see if there was any news of work. A fresh water haul was being assembled with a possible start this afternoon. The dispatcher assured us we would be the only company on the project giving us five days of steady work. We used the morning to make repairs on trucks and stock up on supplies. At 1 p.m. we all received a text message with the name of the well and directions to find it. The location was good with a short haul from two different fresh water depots. Twelve trucks headed out in a line almost a half mile long for the hour and a half drive.

The first night went well with a steady flow of trucks cycling the short distance. Spirits were high as we all counted in our heads the dollars we were making. Since this was a five-day exclusive assignment I felt comfortable stopping at midnight to sleep. I set the alarm for 5 a.m. and tucked into the bunk for an extra-long rest.

The next morning a pre-dawn breakfast of microwave eggs and precooked sausage was washed down with fresh coffee I brewed in a tiny two cup pot I had purchased at a truck stop. This was my favorite sleeping spot on the reservation. A small, quiet, older well tucked behind a hill that protected me from the lights and noise of the paved road. In this location, I usually slept well although usually not this long. In high spirits, I pulled onto the road to rejoin the fresh water haul. Turning into the water depot to fill up the tanker I was surprised to see trucks from other companies drawing water. There must be another fresh water haul to another well pad nearby that we hadn't heard about. The eight-mile drive to my delivery location was jammed with trucks and then I realized they were all turning at the same road I was headed to. I had to wait at the Poseidon tank for an unloading slot to open so I could push my water into the tank. Something had changed overnight. This job was no longer exclusive to our company. The pusher could only say that somewhere in the oil company hierarchy a decision had been made to accelerate this haul and more companies had been called in. Trucks were lined up at both the loading and unloading point and the Poseidon tank was filling fast. There was no way this would last five days. We all jumped in to grab as many loads as we could, trying to harvest as much income as possible before this was over.

The dispatcher called mid-morning and asked if he could bring Ron, the new guy, out to ride with me and learn the process. Another person inside the truck would be an intrusion on my life of solitude and with the frustration of this haul becoming a free for all I wasn't in a very good mood. Sure, I had been lonely out here for months, but that didn't mean I was willing to put up with anyone else's opinions within my own tiny world. Grudgingly I agreed to be a trainer for the day. The dispatcher arrived with Ron in mid-afternoon. He was a decent guy and we managed polite conversation in between my lessons to him on how to haul fresh water.

By 7 p.m. the Poseidon tank was full and the pusher sent us all home. The money had been good for one day but this fiasco was telling me something wasn't right in the business office. There wasn't enough work for all the drivers and it was starting to happen more often. New drivers, new trucks and new companies were arriving in the Bakken almost daily, drawn by nationwide reports of a modern day gold rush in oil. Steve had been out here two years and Stewart had been running the company for four. It appeared to me the peak of the boom was in sight. Drilling would continue at a frenzied pace, but the resources to support drilling were catching up to the demand. The free for all of a boom would soon become a wrestling pit of competition.

As I drove home, with Ron in the passenger seat, God silently said, again, "You can go home." This time I was ready to believe and accept this as clear direction.

Back at the shop I cleaned up, ate some dinner and got out my laptop to search flight options. Just before 11 p.m., I walked to Stewart's cabin. He never sleeps for some reason and I could see the television was flickering. When I knocked on the door he yelled from his recliner to come in. He didn't get out of the chair or turn down the volume on the television. Citing undefined issues at home I told Stewart I needed to leave the next day. I couldn't outright quit because I didn't know what was next so I apologized for leaving on short notice and soft-pedaled a likely return. I went back to the truck and booked my airline reservation online to depart the next morning. Before I fell asleep I suddenly realized why the Wyzetta #7 assignment ended in only three days. Just as I had thought at the time, that assignment was an immediate reward for Obedience. What I missed when it ended so quickly was the realization that my oil field experience had run its course. I wasn't pulled off that well so I could sit in the yard for the next test. God had sent a replacement to the well so I could go home. The first phase of my exile was finished.

Ron had nothing else to do the next morning and was happy to drive me to the airport an hour away. As I sorted and packed personal belongings from inside the Freightliner cab I had to decide what to do with the heavy parka the dispatcher had given me the first night. Realizing I had forgotten to pay him the seventy dollars he wanted I started to walk to the office to return the coat. As I climbed down from the truck I saw Ron, and could see this coat was his size. I threw the heavy parka inside his truck and told him he owed the dispatcher seventy dollars for the coat. I hoped I would never see it again.

10

It was now the third week in June. I had been in the oil field exactly four months broken by two short trips home. Flying out that morning I desperately wanted to never come back but I didn't actually have an alternate plan for income. The resort project in Belize was still showing no signs of life. Sixteen months had come and gone since I first connected and they still did not have development money. Before the oil field I had tried to land a job through the online method of searching jobs and uploading resumes. For months I had failed to secure even one interview and only a few rejection responses. Most of the applications and resumes I submitted just disappeared into cyberspace and generated nothing in return. My first day home I opened another online job search and quickly remembered how thoroughly discouraging the job hunting process could be.

Reluctantly, I turned to the truck driver want ads. It seemed to be the only place a former business owner could find work. A trucking job based locally would allow me to be home every night but would not pay very well. The best pay was over the road but that meant being gone in three-week stretches. I needed something unique that would pay top dollar and get me home more often. One ad caught my eye and I called immediately. Two days later, I interviewed with Stan, the owner, who offered me the job in that meeting. The following Monday I reported to work at trucking job number two.

My new employer supplied golf cars in large numbers to support behind the scenes staff and customer rentals at large events. Organizers at events, like an outdoor music fest, a state fair or a big rally, need to move hundreds of staff people and visitors around large venues. Our job was to provide them with a fleet of golf cars to use for the few days of the event. When the event was over we moved the cars to another venue to support a different event.

The first item of orientation was teaching me that these are golf cars, not carts. "A cart," the owner emphatically instructed, "is a small vehicle pushed or pulled by a human or an animal. A self-propelled vehicle, like we rent, is a car." This was important to him, apparently stressed by his father who started the business. This company had more than twelve hundred golf cars of various configurations from two passengers up to six passengers. They had mini work trucks with seats for two people in front of a dump bed like a mini dump truck. There were flatbed golf car trucks to haul gear and specialized golf car trucks marked as mini ambulances to carry injured persons to an infirmary. They even had special golf cars with trailers to haul the mountains of trash an event generated.

The company operated four tractor trailer rigs using custom built trailers that could carry up to twenty-four golf cars in each load. The work was spread over the entire western half of the nation from Minnesota to California and Texas to Oregon. The other three drivers covered mostly western states. Stan said I would operate in a hub and spoke fashion driving out and back from the company's main office in Denver. The assignment should have me home every other night most of the time. He showed me a white Freightliner in good condition which would serve as my new home on the road.

The golf cars were very light loads and the driving was always on paved roads. Driving the cars on and off the truck was nothing like the physical work of loading an oil field tanker. The work was seasonal, from spring through early fall, because no one holds an outdoor event in winter. What a change from the oil field. No rough roads, no mud, no ice. Most of the driving would be daytime with only an occasional need for a night shift and I didn't need any fire proof clothing or winter layers. This had the potential to be a reasonable income producer minus almost everything that made the oil field so miserable.

The weather was beautiful on the last Monday of June as I prepared my new ride for our inaugural trip together. Wearing shorts and a comfortable short sleeve shirt in the spring sunshine I learned the fine art of getting twenty-four golf cars onto the custom trailer. The cars had to be loaded a certain way to make them all fit. The little dump trucks were too wide to go side by side unless one went in facing backward beside another that faced forward. The first two cars on the upper deck had to extend out beyond the front of the trailer, toward the cab of the truck, to make room for all the cars that had to fit on top. On the bottom deck, the last two cars would hang out slightly beyond the rear of the trailer. The loaded rig was an unusual sight that attracted a lot of looks on the highway and a few questions in the truck stops.

The first trip took me to the state fairgrounds in eastern South Dakota. A wonderful drive on a wide two lane highway through western Nebraska displayed new terrain I had never visited. The music on my smart phone had been expanded to six Christian albums and the owner had installed a new stereo in this truck just last week. The cruise control was not working but they assured me the parts were on order and it would be fixed when I returned. The run to South Dakota was ten hours of easy driving. After the conditions of the oil field, this was almost a vacation.

The fairgrounds buzzed with the activity of hundreds of workers setting up a farm and implement show that would start in two days. Stan was staying on site in his motorhome to oversee the rental of more than 200 golf cars at this event. A young man in his mid-twenties who appeared to be a fellow employee was parking the golf cars in neat rows as I brought them off the truck. Stan invited us both to join him for a dinner of barbeque chicken and corn on the cob from his grill. He introduced me to the other employee, Jeff, with the title of transportation manager. Jeff would keep track of the trucks and drivers to coordinate their movements. He would be the one to tell me which types of cars to take to each event and he would be my point of contact for any issues. We shared small talk over dinner and I began to learn the details of a golf car rental business.

We were parked adjacent to the fairgrounds' RV Park which had a nice community restroom with free hot showers. After dinner, I used the clean shower house to wash off the light grime of a work day before I climbed into my Freightliner for a good night sleep. This far north in late spring the weather was perfect. I did not need the truck engine for either heat or cooling. I slept comfortably with the windows down, lulled by the gentle sound of crickets here in farm country. At sunrise the next morning, I left the fairgrounds with an empty trailer for the ten-hour return trip to Denver.

Before the sun set on the second day I had picked up another load of golf cars at the Denver office and driven the one-hour trip south to my home where Mary was waiting with dinner on the patio. The loaded truck was parked in our front pasture ready for an easy trip to New Mexico tomorrow. I fell asleep in my own bed feeling content at this huge leap forward in life. The money was nowhere near what I made as a business owner but it was better than being unemployed. I had survived the oil field and although I did not understand where that house in Belize was going to fit in my life, for now moving golf cars around the country seemed like a good interim step.

The next two weeks continued on the same track. One trip loaded with golf cars followed by one trip empty. The loaded trips were light weight and the empty trips were smooth and fast. This company was busy with events all over the western states. I met another driver who lived in Denver and seemed to run about half of his trips on the west coast and half helping me in the Midwest. Joe was approximately my age but not married and he was happy to be out on the road for weeks at a time. In the world of trucking, this was an easy assignment. Like most over the road truckers, we were paid by the mile. More miles in a day means more income and the boss encouraged us to push to the limit on both our speed and on how many hours we drove each day. Through the peak summer season the company needed to move a lot of golf cars to a lot of places. We racked up thousands of miles each week which translated to good income for work that was really pretty easy.

Jeff communicated entirely by text message and those were short. He would send a text to a driver with a short list of which cars needed to be moved, an address to pick up and an address to deliver. Selecting which highways to travel was up to each driver. Every driver would send Jeff a three or four word text each day giving him an update on location and progress. Jeff responded to our reports with his trademark single letter answer, "K." His abbreviation for the standard acknowledgment of "okay," became our friendly joke back and forth.

A large number of the thousands of visitors and hundreds of staff at each event would often live, temporarily, in recreational vehicles at RV parks either on site or very near the venue. Their temporary city would include clean restrooms with hot showers to support their camping life. When I delivered or picked up golf cars I would finish all of the work then enjoy a shower and clean clothes immediately prior to climbing in the cab for the next drive. Compared to the barren existence of life in the oil field, access to a hot shower in a clean bathhouse every day was a real blessing.

This truck was in better shape and slightly newer than what I had left behind in North Dakota. In addition to the refrigerator, microwave and coffee pot this home on wheels also included a memory foam mattress on the bed and clean, carpeted floors. The new stereo filled my days with praise music blasting through an eight-speaker surround sound that rattled the windows as I traveled. There was no mud, I didn't have to hang up wet, dirty coveralls at night and my clothes did not smell like diesel fuel.

Exile: A Modern Wilderness Journey

Driving on real highways among real civilization took me to truck stops for fuel where I discovered they had driver loyalty programs. The company credit card paid for the hundreds of gallons of diesel fuel my journeys consumed but the loyalty points were credited to my personal rewards account. Those points paid for hot coffee, fresh pizza and a constant supply of the crumb-covered doughnuts that had become my evening addiction. Whenever possible I tried to buy fuel and rack up points at one particular national chain of truck stops where they served pizza as delicious as any restaurant.

Late spring rolled into mid-summer with the landscape of America scrolling past my windshield. Stan's original plan of running a hub and spoke out of Denver was not working as well as we had hoped. I moved cars between South Dakota and Minnesota for a week before making it home for two nights. That was still better than the oil field that kept me out a month or more. Twice in July I was able to park the loaded truck at home overnight and slept in my own bed before making the one-day trip to New Mexico and back. Those were the only two times our plan of getting me home every other night ever worked.

I continued to deny any identification as a truck driver. If friends or family asked what I was doing I referred to this as my summer job, acting as if I was semi-retired and this was an alternative to golf. Over the road trucker was not, in my mind, a better job title or identity than oil field trucker had been. But, with the greatly improved living conditions of this job I no longer felt I was in exile. As an interim step in life I was able to accept this until I could resume my life as a business man building homes in the Caribbean. Life had gotten much easier and I was cruising on autopilot expecting God to flip the switch back to my dream of life in Belize at any moment. Periodic emails from the Belize resort project assured me they were making progress on their funding which would lead to the project manager position for me. A life in the Caribbean seemed to still be developing it was just taking longer than I wanted. "Probably by the start of the next dry season in January I could be back to where I wanted to be," I told myself.

This was an easy routine with only two drawbacks. The beautiful scenery and interesting venues were a great travel opportunity but I missed Mary. She would have been welcome to ride along and see the country but Mary operated her own business and we have horses, a dog and a big garden at home. The logistics of life, especially in summer, made it impossible for her to hit the open road with me. The second problem was my growing boredom with life on the highway. After the novelty of this new adventure wore off I found myself sitting for hours each day enduring endless and monotonous highway driving. The cruise control had been repaired and was now set every day at seventy-two miles per hour as mile after mile after mile of highway rolled under the wheels.

Crossing the western states in an air-conditioned cab wearing shorts, a T-shirt and sneakers was as stress free as any job I could imagine. Compared to the oil field I was cruising, literally, on easy street. Praise music from the stereo filled the cab, but I had not heard a word from God in more than two months. Important life questions that seemed so pressing in the oil field had slipped from my mind in this environment of benign monotony. The only stirring in my soul was a growing restlessness and impatience woven through the hours of driving.

Exile: A Modern Wilderness Journey

In early August, one of the four company trucks suffered a serious mechanical breakdown on the west coast. Losing that unit was causing the west coast operation to fall behind schedule. Jeff asked if I was willing to go out further from home and stay out for more days at a time to help maintain the schedule until the truck was repaired. Knowing this was a seasonal job with only a few weeks left, I was willing to take the increased miles that translated into bigger paychecks.

My first trip outside the original hub and spoke plan took me west through the beauty of the Colorado Mountains in summer. I was on my way to Las Vegas with twenty-two of the little dump truck cars to be used at a big car racing event. The highway wound through Glenwood Canyon alongside the Colorado River on one of the most scenic routes in America. This was longer than any trip I had made so far, driving more hours each day and extending the number of days I would be away from home.

Before I left that morning, Mary and I discussed ideas to deal with the long hours of boredom. An internet search introduced me to the world of podcasts which I had heard of but never experienced. Similar to radio but delivered over the Internet, podcasts were available on demand through an app downloaded to my phone. I never understood people's interest in talk radio, but this was more like teaching. It looked like this might be similar to attending a class or a lecture. We found thousands of teachers and speakers covering just about every imaginable topic. Maybe I could use the hours alone in the cab to learn something useful.

The evening sun was barely below the western horizon as the interstate highway moved away from the winding river that defines Glenwood Canyon. Straight highway and relatively flat land lay before me and I should have good cell phone reception for at least an hour. My first opportunity to experience podcast technology opened with the familiar voice of a Bible preacher I had not heard in three decades. The soothing tone and perfectly paced delivery of Chuck Swindoll flowed over the internet, through cell towers, into my smartphone and filled the cab of the truck just as stars began to twinkle in the clear night sky.

Through the remainder of the summer and into early fall the technology of cell phones and podcasts brought Insight for Living Ministries into my constantly moving work/home combination. I searched the podcast offerings and added Greg Laurie's Harvest Ministries to my daily routine. Both men's teachings were stimulating and brought a fresh element to life in a truck. Their voices were life within the solitude of the highway. Searching through the hundreds of podcasters available I found the teachings of an Orthodox Christian priest which brought a new perspective and an historical depth to my learning. Father Tom seemed an unlikely participant in this modern technology but his teaching was fascinating as his sermons rambled down dozens of rabbit trails. He had such depth of knowledge I was challenged to listen and try my best to follow his long, rambling lectures, to pull out nuggets of new knowledge.

My life inside the truck developed a pattern that began most days before sunrise in the parking lot of some random, crowded truck stop. The cell phone alarm would awaken me and, after dressing and making the bed, I would withdraw the blackout curtains covering the windows and rejoin the truck stop world with the sounds and lights and movement of hundreds of trucks and truckers. At the end of each day I would fall asleep in the parking lot of a different truck stop surrounded, again, by the noise and lights and movement of hundreds of trucks. The cab of the truck was transformed each night from work to home by sliding blackout curtains I could pull on a sliding track over the windows to close off the outside world and create my private retreat. Between sunrise and sunset, the constant rumble of the diesel engine underscored my reclusive life of praise music, Bible teaching and contemplation.

God had not given me any revelations about what to call this phase of life. Unlike that night in the blizzard when exile was identified, I had no specific name for what was happening here. Life was still not what I wanted it to be and for that reason I was not completely opposed to the isolation. Trying to explain this to anyone else was something I couldn't have done and didn't want to try.

My living and working conditions had improved enormously compared to the oil field, but I continued to be alone day after day. Once each day I might exchange a polite hello and thank you with a cashier when I bought fuel and food at a truck stop. Every afternoon my five word text to Jeff would receive the expected response of "K." Delivering or picking up golf cars at venues did not require discussion with anyone. As soon as I arrived at a new location I could easily spot the parking lot filled with hundreds of golf cars and either take what I came for or add what I was delivering. My paperwork did not require any signatures from the customer and they were too busy with their event to give more than a polite nod if they even noticed me driving in and out.

In the first week of adding the podcast format I discovered something called the Daily Audio Bible. Each day the founder, Brian Hardin, would read portions of the Bible. He started January first with Genesis 1 and would read through the entire Bible in one year. Each day covered a portion of the Old Testament, a portion of the New Testament, a Psalm and a few Proverbs. Listening to Brian's voice as he read with understanding and clarity was as if I was sitting beside a campfire in ancient Israel hearing Moses teach the history of Israel. Bible stories I had heard many times in my life, but never fully understood, suddenly opened up in waves of successive revelation.

I had found DAB in August which meant they were eight months ahead of me, but I had lots of time to fill. The podcast format let me go back and start at the January first podcast and I could listen to five or six podcasts each day. God's Word came off the printed pages I had seen all my life and became a living part of my days inside that white Freightliner.

My routine would cycle through a few hours alternating between music and teaching, then a stop for either fuel, food or a few minutes of housekeeping, followed by a short nap. Rested and refueled, the cycle would repeat, usually about four hours at a time. At some point in late afternoon, usually around sunset, I would be weary of the constant sounds of truck noise, the wind and the stereo whether it was music or teaching. Switching the radio off, I would take an hour or so with only the road noise to process my thoughts.

Exile: A Modern Wilderness Journey

The changed driving plan had taken me far beyond the original hub and spoke operation that was supposed to be based from Denver. This new, hectic pace carried me through Denver that month for barely an hour. Instead, my routes became long mileage runs like three days driving from New Mexico to Oregon, then two days from Oregon to Minnesota and then three days to California. East then west, north to south, I crisscrossed eighteen western states moving golf cars at a frantic pace. After the one company truck had broken down in California that driver was arrested on outstanding warrants that Stan didn't know about when he hired the driver. This season would soon be over and Stan was trying to avoid hiring a new driver so close to winter shutdown but that meant we were all pushing our limits to accomplish the work of four trucks using only three. For a few days, Jeff and I shared my truck moving cars to the annual motorcycle rally in Sturgis, South Dakota. The South Dakota state fair in Huron was finished which left us with four hundred golf cars that needed to move to Sturgis. I would make a twelve hour round-trip over Interstate 90 to deliver twenty-four cars and get back to Huron at sundown. Jeff and I would re-load the truck with a new set of cars and he would drive the round trip to Sturgis and back over night while I slept in a camping trailer at the fairgrounds. When he rolled back into Huron at sunrise we loaded the truck again and I headed west with another load. This trucking round robin went on for four days until we had enough cars moved to get the Sturgis operation back on schedule. On the opening day of the annual rally the streets of Sturgis were jammed with thousands of motorcycles moving slowly through the small town. In the midst of that chaos, I rolled slowly through the crowded streets with a loaded semi delivering the last twenty-four cars to round out our total of seven hundred on site, one of the company's biggest events.

After Sturgis, the focus of the company moved to the west coast. We moved load after load after load of golf cars to Idaho and Oregon and California and Nevada in a flurry of trips, dispatched by Jeff with his simple text messages.

Driving across the vast, open land of southeastern Oregon for the first time in my life, I listened to Brian read from the book of Mathew. I heard the words of Jesus in a tone and an understanding that had never hit me so clearly before. I had read those words, or heard them preached, so many times over the past fifty years they had to be woven in to the fabric of my being, and yet these familiar sayings suddenly came across as if they were new. Through the Gospels I was being told to seek and ask and knock. Jesus was admonishing me to store up treasures in heaven and serve only one master. This teaching was familiar but I had never fit the segments all together like they were fitting out here on this empty two lane highway. My understanding shifted from a simple acknowledgement of "seek," which to me had always meant go looking, to a new understanding of "SEEK!," which meant search like your life depends on it. Jesus was not telling us to engage in a casual search or a study one night a week for six weeks. He was clearly and emphatically telling me to pursue heaven as my single most important reason for living. Sell everything. Surrender everything. Free myself from the world and devote myself to discovering and attaining the kingdom of Heaven!

As podcasts from a half dozen leading teachers streamed across my speakers the teaching of the New Testament began to fit together with the history of the Old Testament. Hearing the whole story unfold with no other distractions, I began to put the entire picture together with clarity and comprehension beyond any understanding I had ever seen before.

Up until a few years ago, when the business pulled me entirely out of the church, I had spent my adult life, and most of my youth, living what I understood to be a Christian life. Bible study in many different forms had been present through most of my adult years and yet never before had I seen the Bible with such depth and brilliance. While I was busy living the American Dream I had failed to grasp what God was trying to communicate.

Brian would often teach for a few minutes after delivering each day's podcast. One day he commented how too many of us spend our time learning *about* God and we never actually *know* God. Our well-intentioned study practices fill us with knowledge but fail to introduce us to the person of God who speaks through blizzards and in truck cabs.

I began to understand the difference between studying the Bible and reading the Bible as a complete story. Study is what we do when we are searching for key verses, specific topics, or comparing Old Testament against New Testament. Studies have a place and a purpose but are usually focused on specific outcomes. Through all of the Sunday morning sermons or Thursday night men's groups over many years I had only taken in bits and pieces of the Bible. Those disjointed pieces had never connected into a big picture for me and were never more than just a subtle undertone to my life. The Daily Audio Bible now brought large chunks of the Bible to my Freightliner cab five times a day in a cascade of comprehension that a lifetime of piecemeal Bible study had never provided. Reading the Bible in large continuous blocks tied all of the study segments together.

Randall L. Cumley

Chasing the American Dream had kept me both entertained and occupied but, while living in that fog of self-centered busyness, I had never realized my Christian beliefs were so fragmented and disjointed. Slowly, over many years, the pressures and distractions of life had pushed the few piecemeal messages of the Bible I had managed to retain onto a dusty back shelf of my life while the distractions and selfishness of secular life drew my attention. Confined now within this steel box rumbling south towards San Diego I had nothing else to do and nowhere else to be. The busyness of life had been removed and the secular distractions were beyond my grasp. The Bible, coming to me over the Internet through faithful teachers, came off that back shelf and moved, for the first time, into the center of my life. Receiving God's teaching in large blocks supported by good instruction brought me into a big picture understanding like I had never known.

In the mountains of northern California Chuck Swindoll delivered a teaching on Joseph I had heard many times in my life, but I had never seen the details the way Chuck taught them that day on U.S 97. The winding two-lane highway cut through a beautiful range of pine forested mountains that provided a magnificent backdrop for Chuck's detailed teaching. A rhythm of moving golf cars, sleeping in a campground or a truck stop, and moving more golf cars began to pass under my wheels almost unnoticed as the cab was filled each day with Scripture and teaching.

This huge volume of Bible study began to intertwine through the questions and challenges I had wrestled with over the past eighteen months.

From wondering why third world laborers bothered to continue their bare subsistence my thoughts expanded to wondering why any humans continued on. I started to ponder if the opportunities and amenities of a first world life were only masking the reality that our affluent lives were a different form of subsistence. Opportunity made life fun while it lasted, but rich and poor were all going to end at the same place facing the same challenge. Chasing the American Dream was a variation of merely surviving until death brought the meaningless folly to an end.

Only a few short years before, my life had included a six-figure income along with the options and toys that much cash flow can provide. Now, with the affluence stripped away, I understood that lifestyle had been an illusion. Without the smoke and mirrors of an American consumer mentality to blind me, I could see my assets and projects and entertainment were only distractions. I had failed to see two critical realities. The first was that I could be a citizen of God's Kingdom on earth right now, with the benefits and privileges that includes, and the second was that I had the opportunity to impact the nature and quality of my eternity.

In the cab of that truck crossing the Utah salt flats I grasped for the first time the parables of the New Testament teaching so clearly about the folly of storing up wealth on this earth. No matter what we accumulate on earth we take nothing with us into the next phase and none of our earthly affluence will directly impact our eternity.

This was not news, the lesson has been publicly available for centuries, and yet the words had never been so clear. Delivered in large uninterrupted blocks with no competing distractions I saw for the first time how the various lessons of the Bible were woven together to form a comprehensive life lesson. Taking in the entire Bible story in large continuous segments showed me the complete picture in a way that years of small studies had never delivered.

While stuck one afternoon in the heavy traffic of Los Angeles I thought of people I know who worked with financial planners to map out their entire life making sure they had enough money to carry them to and through retirement. Often they had gone so far as planning and funding their own funeral. Some had even set aside specific resources to pay the final bill that would lower their flesh into the ground. Remembering these discussions as I drove caused me to question out loud, "then what?" They had covered every detail up to the absolute last minute of their life on earth but ignored what would happen after that. How could anyone disregard Jesus' direction that we should, and could, store up treasures in heaven? He told us we have the ability to affect both the direction and the quality of our individual eternity and He encouraged us to exercise that opportunity!

The Old Testament so clearly instructed the Children of Israel how they could determine their own daily quality of life as God shared statements of If/Then. IF they would follow His instruction, THEN they would be blessed. IF they chose to go their own way THEN they would be subject to curse. In the New Testament, Jesus told us plainly that the road to life is narrow and only a few will find it. Finding the narrow road and narrow gate are active tasks He was encouraging us to engage in. Finding only happens when we search. He had given me a call to action far beyond simple church membership and daily devotionals.

Jesus told us we can affect the outcome of how we transition from this life to the next. If we seek, if we ask, if we search, we can and will find the narrow gate. We have the ability to ascend the narrow path. This is up to us. "Why have I invested my energies and talents into chasing after boats and vacations and fancy dinners and toys and distractions when I could have been investing in my eternity," I wondered. How had I missed something so clear that had been in front of me for so many years?

My questions about life that started in Belize began to turn around one hundred eighty degrees as I realized subsistence was not a problem, it was a blessing. Those poor workers invested themselves in family and community. They built relationships with each other. They had time and mental energy to develop the personal traits Jesus was encouraging. They had the opportunity to love one another.

Fourteen months ago I asked God to explain why a third-world laborer would continue in a life that appeared to have no purpose. God responded by stripping away my first-world disguise and exposing that I should be asking myself the question, "Why do I continue my masquerade of affluence?" As a typical American I was working way too much just to support a life of selfish entertainment. I didn't have the time, the desire or the understanding to develop meaningful relationships with the people in my life, and I certainly was not investing in my eternity.

That spring I watched the farmers in South Dakota tilling their ground as soon as the winter frost was gone. Over the summer, in States across the nation, I saw seedlings emerge from sun-warmed soil, then grow, flower and set fruit. Through the windshield of a truck, I watched the annual cycle of tilling, planting, watering and nurturing of crops from Minnesota to California. As the harvest of crops and the changing of leaves peaked across America the teachings within my cab seemed to have completed a cycle of their own.

Randall L. Cumley

Hours and hours of focused study had brought me to the realization that acknowledging what will happen after I die is the key to understanding what I should be doing while I live. Until I resolved, accepted and committed to an understanding about life after death I was unknowingly wasting my life before death.

I came to believe that my entire existence on this earth is for the purpose of training and preparing for the eternity that will follow my short mortal experience. After thousands of miles of driving provided me hundreds of hours of teaching I saw for the first time in my life that this earthly existence is intended to be a prelude to eternity. A prelude that will establish the tone and quality of my forever life. In the short time I have for this phase of life I should be focused on developing into the person God created me to be *for eternity*. Becoming that person should be my most important task in this first phase of human life.

Contrary to my original question about why poor people would continue what I thought were desolate lives, I now had to ask why affluent people devoted our lives to chasing meaningless experiences and useless vanity while our single biggest opportunity, the chance to direct our eternity, is either pushed to the sideline as a minor part of life or, even worse, ignored entirely.

This new understanding of life's meaning was so overwhelming I had to stop at a scenic overlook and absorb the revelation. On a beautiful evening in the mountains of western Utah, surrounded by the colors of the rocky, red cliffs at sunset, I took a break from the noise and motion of the truck. I sat in silence on a rock wall with a stunning view of a river below allowing my soul a few minutes to grasp this new understanding of the central theme of life. I realized the process of growing into the person God created me to be is a full time task I will barely be able to complete in the few years I have available before I transition to eternity. My only hope for finding the narrow path that will lead me into a successful eternity depends on my personal effort to overcome the distractions of daily life while seeking the eternity God has designed specifically for me.

As my mind worked through the expanded understanding of life being created by the volumes of material I was absorbing each day, I realized God was once again speaking to me in between the teachings flowing into my cab via podcast.

Crossing Nevada on Interstate 80 I asked God why previous business efforts had not been successful. When we built that waterpark in northern Colorado, Mary and I were deeply involved in our local church. As a family, we were committed to prayer and as owners we were leading the management employees of the business in daily prayer and bible study. "Why had that not resulted in business success to underwrite our faith," I asked out loud. In His nanosecond style God told me, "You weren't ready."

I repeated the answer in my mind, "You weren't ready." That business had crumbled, our life was turned upside down and we headed off in a different direction because I wasn't ready. Instinctively, I understood what He meant was that if the waterpark had been successful I would have been distracted by everything that is the world. At best, the success would have prevented me from ever discovering what I was learning right now. At worst, the success might have destroyed my life and my family by giving me access to distractions that would have denied me any spiritual growth.

Digging deeper into what that revelation meant, I realized the lessons now filling my cab had always been around me and other people were receiving them but I had missed the big picture. In those years of trying to be what I thought was faithful; I had been trying to draft God as a partner in my plans. I had never grasped the concept of surrendering my own ideas in order to pursue His route to victory. More importantly, I was working with a wrong definition of victory. I had been chasing success as defined by the American Dream. That vision of success is very short-sighted and pursues a goal that is only temporary, measured in earthly values. God's definition of success is achieved when we cross over from mortality into eternity with Him. I had been blind to that definition of success, for more than three decades.

"What about traffic control," I asked. That business idea developed out of lunch with a pastor. Why didn't that lead to success to support a Christian family? As soon as that question crossed my lips, I immediately realized I did not need God to answer that question. My own actions had demonstrated, to myself and everyone around me, that I was not ready for worldly success. If the initial success of that business had continued I would have buried my own eternity under an expensive avalanche of false ideals and secular distractions. By ending that business and transitioning to the physical labor and cultural challenge of Belize, God had opened a door for me to be redirected into a life focused on eternity instead of focused on earth.

As I headed east on Interstate 8 between San Diego and Phoenix, God added a new twist in my education. Driving through the wind-blown desert adjacent to the Mexico border, my mind was seared with the realization that the human story of the Bible was still progressing and my life was a part of the story currently being written. Before that day I always understood the Bible as a history lesson. I had never considered that the story was still in progress with me as a character.

On the last day of September I made it home again after driving more miles in one month than I ever imagined was possible. An unusual three-day break was wonderful including an opportunity for Mary and I to join close friends at a favorite restaurant for dinner and some long overdue social interaction.

Everyone at this table knew me well, including that I displayed traits of attention deficit disorder. Sitting still to study had always been difficult for me. As I was sharing stories of moving golf cars from point A to point B and talking about the many podcasts I had absorbed, we almost simultaneously smiled at the realization of what God had done.

The summer of hauling golf cars had been God's beautifully orchestrated method of providing an education I could never have accomplished through conventional schooling. My entire value system was being rewritten through a process God had arranged specifically for my attention deficit brain. The questions raised in Belize had made the summer's study topics deeply interesting. Alone in the cab of a truck I had no distractions and no options that would allow me to leave the air ride seat of His classroom. I could not choose to skip a lesson to go clean the garage or aimlessly surf the internet. In order to make a living I had to be driving. The absence of contact with other people eliminated the entanglements of personal relationships that might have disrupted His teaching. Hours of monotonous driving kept my brain available to process and absorb the material He presented. This was possibly the only place on the planet where I could earn a living and simultaneously soak in God's lessons in an environment of no distractions.

God had literally strapped me into a seat, cleared my calendar and poured His word, His teaching and His answers directly into my soul. As I drove that truck around the United States my mind did not have to compete with the noise and distractions of life. I was relieved of decisions and released from most obligations. Each day for four solid months I had only two tasks, drive the truck and listen to God speak. The bare existence and isolation of trucking had made possible the most important education I would ever receive.

13

By mid-October, the outdoor event season was over. We had a final two weeks of cleanup as we gathered cars from finished events and moved them back to Denver for the winter. I was exhausted from so much driving and so many days on the road. I was ready for a break so I flew to Belize to invest two weeks making a small amount of progress on my house.

The big resort project still lacked money to start work but they were sending me regular email updates expressing their hope for a financial breakthrough and still offering me a job as project manager. In their process of searching for funding, they crossed paths with two men who recently bought land to launch a small development of spec homes. Robert and John had purchased ten lots on a small street behind my house. They were anxious to start construction immediately on houses to sell in the same middle price range I was targeting. Their concept was almost exactly the same as what I had started two years prior. However, they faced an immediate problem of a complete lack of construction experience. Neither of them knew a hammer from a skid loader. They needed expertise to build these houses and I was recommended to them by the developer at the resort project. We met over dinner and discussed their project. Three days later I flew home to Colorado boasting a new job title. I had landed my first official job as a construction management consultant. These two men were willing to pay me to oversee the design and construction of their spec houses. It appeared my exile was over and the Belize life could continue.

Working with a Belize architect, I put together designs for the first three houses which earned me an income for the first three months of the year. Within a few weeks, I discovered these two had a lot of ideas but not nearly enough money. Plans for construction stopped abruptly when they could not assemble a financing package for their project. Exactly the same issue the big resort had run into, a grand idea but no money to execute. Consulting turned out to be a very short career.

The oil boom in the had Bakken collapsed in the spring of 2015 as oil prices tumbled. Steve had found a new job in Fargo, North Dakota through a friend and he was kind enough to include me. I would again be wrestling with an identity crisis trying my hardest to avoid accepting the idea that truck driver was my occupation and I would, again, be away from home for weeks at a time living in the isolation of a truck cab.

The summer and fall of 2015 slid by, completely uneventful, as I drove a consistent three thousand mile round trip from Fargo to the east coast and back. Nothing of great interest happened during this period either in the driving or the teaching. This assignment was a repetitive route over the same highways and sleeping in the same truck stops week after week. I continued to listen to Daily Audio Bible and podcasts of great teachers but God provided no new revelations. This summer was, apparently, a plateau in my training allowing me to rest before God carried me in to one final trucking assignment He had planned.

The first three trucking jobs each involved a dedicated truck that became my personal space. In each truck I had food, spare clothing, books and a comfortable bed. An important part of keeping my sanity during the isolation of these jobs was to make the truck as much of a home as possible. A real mattress made up with sheets and blankets brought a sense of normal to the night. During the day I kept the bed neatly made and the truck well organized. In the oil field, the life was challenging but I had my home around me, as neat and tidy as I could make it. When I was moving golf cars I could stop each night and cocoon inside my personal space. The top of the line Kenworth I drove hauling windows was downright luxurious. That truck was quiet to drive all day and comfortable at night, as nice inside as any motorhome.

Having my home around me inside the cab allowed me to establish a small personal safety net of preparation. To be ready for any event I never let the fuel tanks get below half and I always had enough food on board to cover a few days. If any calamity disrupted the normal routine, whether it was a mechanical breakdown, weather or an accident, I was prepared to wait it out. Preparing and carrying supplies gave me a sense of control over my life within the cab. I would soon discover God had trucking assignment number four planned to yank that rug of self-dependence out from under my life.

Randall L. Cumley

March of 2016 started our fourth consecutive year with no financial stability and nothing coming together. Mary and I wondered out loud at dinner one night, "How long can this go on?" I could have returned to Fargo and another year of hauling windows to the east coast but the boredom of hours on the highway combined with weeks of time away from home was, for us, the definition of a life not worth living. Life in a velvet rut would be the best description. The job would produce a livable income but neither of us would enjoy the lifestyle. If life was nothing more than hours and days and weeks of isolation in the cab of a truck while Mary lived alone in Colorado, why go on no matter how good the income? It was a life of separation and we did not want to continue that way if we could find another option.

Searching, again, through the truck driver want ads I found a concept I had not seen before. The task was moving trucks between locations for various customers. Every day there were dozens of trucks being moved from a seller to a buyer or within a company from one hub to another. The trucks were empty or without a trailer and every imaginable type of truck was being moved. The work was done as an independent contractor and there were several brokers who provided this service to customers by managing a team of drivers. Through phone calls, online applications and faxed contracts I connected with two different brokers. Once I was in their system I could look at their online dispatch boards to find the trucks that needed to move and see if the configuration matched my preferences. As an independent contractor I would be paid a flat rate per mile for moving the truck. All expenses came out of my pocket. Every penny I could save on expenses increased the amount I had left over to pay bills at home. The concept in this business was to travel bare bones in order to maximize income. Even the fuel burned in the truck was an expense the drivers had to pay which motivated the drivers to manage their fuel costs.

To start the first trip, I booked a flight from Denver to Dallas for forty-four dollars. From the Dallas airport, I had an Uber driver take me to the truck pickup point. This was an empty vacuum tanker just like the truck I operated in the Bakken. This truck had been sold by an oil company in Texas that had gone bankrupt from the drop in oil price. A different oil company in Pennsylvania was still operating and they bought twelve identical trucks through the bankruptcy auction. They hired my broker to move the trucks from Texas to Pennsylvania and the broker hired me. When the Uber driver dropped me at the truck I had one very small suitcase I had carried on the airplane that contained fresh socks and underwear, two T-shirts a sleeping bag and a pillow. The clothes I was wearing completed my supplies for what I anticipated would be a two-week assignment.

The used truck waiting to be moved was in good condition and it had a sleeper cab which meant I would not have to get a motel room. I threw my suitcase in the truck, did an inspection to be sure everything worked and that the truck was safe then I headed to the closest truck stop for fuel. If this was going to be profitable I had to be sure I did not buy too much fuel, only enough to get the truck to the delivery point. I did not want to deliver the truck with fuel in the tank that I had paid for. My paperwork told me the expected miles to the destination and I could estimate generally what a truck like this would consume per mile so I made a fuel calculation and bought slightly less than that amount. After I had traveled a thousand or so miles in this specific truck I would be able to accurately calculate the final leg of the trip and put in just enough fuel to coast into the customer's yard on fumes.

This was a three-day, two-night trip and having the sleeper cab would save me the cost of two nights in a motel. Late in the afternoon on the third day, I parked the truck in Pottstown, gave the keys to the new owner and summoned an Uber driver who raced through rush hour traffic to get me to the Philadelphia airport. Another cheap airline ticket took me back to Dallas where I had to pay for a room overnight. At dawn on day four, a third Uber driver took me to the original truck yard to start my second run. I was competing against other independent drivers working through the same broker to get these jobs. If I moved quickly I hoped I might be able to get three of the twelve trucks moved before the opportunity was gone. The second truck was a little cleaner and a little nicer than the first and this truck had more than a half a tank of fuel which was money in my pocket! I hit the highway in high spirits and headed east toward Arkansas.

The broker had supplied me with state license plates to be duct taped to the front of the truck. In the passenger window I taped a placard that showed this truck was being moved by a licensed transport agent. Driving through Tennessee the second day, I called my broker to see if I could find a truck that needed to leave Pennsylvania, where I was headed. This broker had nothing pending in the area so I called a second broker to check his options. He had a truck about forty miles from my destination and it needed to go to Dallas but it would not be ready to go for another day. That was perfect. I could drop the truck I was in and get paid to take a different truck back to Dallas.

I reached the town of delivery in the second truck about three in the afternoon on day six. The customer had not set any specific delivery times and I did not want to spend money on a motel so I parked behind a bowling alley one block away from the delivery and slept in the truck for the night. For dinner I had a really bad burger at the bowling alley bar and grill and then went to bed with a stomach ache. This transient life of jumping from truck to truck meant I could not carry extra food or supplies. Each day I would buy enough food for that day. I could not keep a cooler to carry food because I didn't want to pay baggage charges on the airlines to move the cooler to the next ride. This would only work if I maintained a bare bones existence. Eating at restaurants, or bowling alleys, would burn up too much income. I needed to trim my food down to what I could carry easily and consume quickly. Granola bars and fruit became my lifestyle.

At sunrise the next morning I delivered the truck I had slept in and summoned another Uber driver who dropped me at a suburban train station. An hour-long train ride to Harrisburg, Pennsylvania was relaxing and scenic then another Uber driver carried my suitcase and me to truck number three. I began to think Uber was going to make more money from this than I was.

The third truck for the week was a day cab "bobtail." That means the truck was only large enough for two seats with no sleeper. The term "bobtail" meant I would not be pulling a trailer; this was just the tractor unit. Reversing the route I had just covered twice in six days, this would be another three-day two-night trip but with no way to sleep in the truck. Motel costs would eat away at my income. The first night I found a room for fifty-five dollars. This was a long, long drop from the way I used to travel. When my business was booming

I stayed in a lot of expensive, fancy hotels in a lot of nice places and I really loved that life. Back then a room for anything less than two hundred dollars a night was below my standard. Now I was shopping online to find a bargain motel beside the highway for fifty dollars a night. Life had truly taken a new turn.

The following day, eleven hours of driving got me to Little Rock, Arkansas and another fifty dollar motel. At check-in I joined the loyalty program for this motel chain to start earning points for room discounts. Signing up for a budget motel rewards program seemed like a cruel reflection back to the days when I was a Gold Member with several luxury hotel chains. After checking in, I drove the bobtail to a self-service laundry, bought a single use packet of detergent from the coin-operated vendor and washed the meager set of clothes I had been wearing for more than a week. As the clothes were spinning in the machine I walked across the street to a convenience store to buy my nightly treat of crumb doughnuts and a carton of milk.

While I waited for the laundry to dry, I checked email and looked at the online broker bulletin boards to see what trucks might be coming up. There was one more tanker waiting to be moved from Dallas to Pennsylvania if I could get there before another independent beat me to it. When the laundry was finished, I drove the bobtail back to the motel on the poor side of Little Rock. A taco shop in front of the motel provided dinner for less than five bucks. I carried laundry and food to the room where I ate my tacos from a Styrofoam to-go box. After a shower, I climbed into bed to enjoy my doughnuts and maybe a half hour of TV to nod off. The air conditioner would rattle for a few minutes until the room was too cold, go silent until the room was too hot and then rattle again. When the air conditioner was off I realized the room smelled like urine. The carpet was seriously overdue for cleaning. I was too tired to go to the office and move to another room. I decided to mentally block out both the smell and the noise and just sleep.

I made it to Dallas by lunchtime the next day and that third tanker I had been hoping to get was still available but it wasn't at the truck yard, it was in a dealership repair shop. Another independent had started to take this truck to Pennsylvania but it broke down in the first ten miles and had to be towed in. The length of time for repairs was unclear so the other driver ditched the assignment and went somewhere else. The truck was supposed to be ready now at the dealership. Another Uber ride took another forty dollars from my bank. I found tractor number four in the dealer's repair lot with the vacuum tanker trailer out on the street. After signing the repair invoice, I connected the tractor to the trailer and was ready to roll just as Dallas/Fort Worth traffic hit peak evening rush hour. Driving a semi, with a thirteen speed manual transmission, through stop and go traffic for two hours was not how I wanted to start this trip but I could not afford to just sit and wait.

Crawling through traffic I used the time to mentally evaluate if this moving trucks concept was working. The good news was this chaos was making money and the pay was direct deposited into my bank each day. The bills at home were getting paid as long as I could continue to live on nearly nothing out here on the road.

As the sun dropped below the horizon behind me on day number ten I was passing through east Texas on my way, again, to Pennsylvania. Two days later I delivered the third and final oil field tanker to its new owner. Uber sent a driver to move my suitcase and me to a depot thirty miles away where brand new tractors from the Mack factory were ready for delivery. A text message on my phone told me to contact the guard shack at the gate to pick up transport paperwork which lead me to a beautiful blue tractor with every option and feature including a brand new mattress and a built in refrigerator. This would be another bobtail, but at least it was a sleeper, going to a truck dealer in Chicago. Coming out of the factory there was less than a gallon of fuel in each of the two tanks. That was not enough fuel to reach a truck stop so I had to maneuver this big truck up to the pumps at the nearest convenience store to get fuel. I grabbed a few food supplies for the two day trip which would take me north to Interstate 80. I slept that night in a familiar truck stop I had visited many times last year when hauling windows.

The dealer in Chicago opened at 8 a.m. on Monday and I was there with the new Mack waiting in the lot. After an inspection and acceptance from the manager, I summoned another Uber driver, my silent, and expensive, partner in this business. Two more trucks, two more Uber drivers and two rental cars carried me from Chicago to St Louis to Denver and then home over the next three days. The second day of that final leg started with a drive through Missouri in a day cab bobtail surrounded by black clouds and sheets of windblown rain. At times the Interstate highway traffic slowed to a crawl because of the intensity of the wind and rain. I had tuned the truck's AM radio to get weather reports and heard a constant stream of computerized weather warnings about severe storms and tornadoes in the counties around me. Buffeted by the wind and pelted with rain and hail, I covered barely thirty miles in the next hour before breaking out of the weather into a clear blue sky and dry highway.

Three hours later, just west of Topeka, Kansas, a second storm, with tremendous lightning and rain by the bucketful, forced me into a rest area along with a dozen other trucks. While I waited for the rain to let up, the AM radio sounded out a tornado alert. The computerized voice from the weather service called out the location and direction of an active tornado and I realized I was sitting at essentially ground zero. "Take cover," was the warning from the radio as the wind rocked my day cab side to side. When I looked around at the rest area parking lot I saw trees bending in the wind but there was no place to take cover. Judging from the wind direction and intensity of the rain my best guess was that the actual tornado was just barely behind me and headed away. Ten minutes later the rain eased up enough that I could return to the interstate headed west. There was a small chance I might make it home that night except the sky ahead looked as black as what I just passed through.

A few miles before crossing from Kansas into Colorado the sun was going down below the horizon under a sky filled with ominous black clouds. From here I could be home in just under three hours but the weather radar on my smartphone was showing a large and very intense storm ahead. Rather than risk driving through potentially the third tornado of the day, which would be even worse in the dark, I grudgingly pulled off the highway and found a motel for the night.

That first trip ran seventeen days where I drove seven different trucks, paid for seven Uber drivers, two airline flights and two rental cars and slept in six cheap motel rooms before my dirty laundry and I made it home. Perhaps because of the novelty of solving a new challenge I was not as discouraged as I should have been. The process had generated enough income to keep our utilities turned on and I had the fun of driving that brand new Mack tractor.

The fun part of this chaos was the chance to drive some really nice new trucks and the scenery which was as beautiful as always. The biggest challenge was moving from truck to truck every few days and living with no reserves. The assignments of the previous years, in the oil field, hauling golf cars or moving windows, always had me in the same truck with all of my possessions. In those jobs life on the road was lonely but at least I was cradled in my own little nest with reserves of food and fuel along with a familiar bed, my books, laptop computer and music. This truck moving was bare-bones trucking decathlon where I jumped from truck to motel to rental car to airplane to Uber to another truck. I had no backup food or personal comforts, often no bed in the truck, and I always operated on minimal fuel hoping to coast into the delivery with empty tanks. I had to balance my expenses on the road against bills at home, a task that consumed the pay just as quickly as it trickled in each day. With no margin and no safety net, my life had become a journey of subsistence completely dependent on God down to the smallest details.

While moving that third vacuum tanker, from Dallas to Pennsylvania, I had awakened one morning before dawn in a truck stop with absolutely no money anywhere in my life. Without enough cash or credit to buy even a cup of coffee I was as broke as the workers in Belize. This job earned enough money each day to pay the bills for that day and I started each morning as broke as I had been the morning before. I had become no different than the workers in Belize whose life had baffled me three years prior. I was working long days in difficult conditions to earn enough money to make it through one more day. There was nothing I could see in this that would ever produce anything greater than just existing.

I had slept the night before in a giant parking lot of more than two hundred idling trucks and I could see the fuel pumps but I could not pull in and buy fourteen gallons of fuel to finish this trip until the broker's office opened for the day and made a deposit to my account. My life had changed from owning a business that ran on multi-year contracts and steady cash flow, to this. In that previous life, I was the boss who made decisions that affected everyone and I directed where the money would flow. I had respect and recognition from employees and clients. Now I was financially broke, humbled and dependent on God for every detail of my life. I was a nobody, going nowhere with nothing.

My hours of driving continued to include the podcasts of Chuck Swindoll and I also subscribed to a daily email devotional from his ministry. This week Chuck was teaching about the life of Moses in the wilderness. Waiting in the truck stop for my funds to be available,

Exile: A Modern Wilderness Journey

I opened the latest email from Chuck Swindoll's Insight for Living Ministries. His teaching on that day was explaining how Moses had been raised in a palace with the privilege and benefits granted to Pharaoh's adopted grandson. A rapid series of events disrupted the royal trajectory of his life and forced Moses into a desert exile. His life changed overnight from being recognized and respected by an entire community to simple days spent alone in a desolate and remote desert. Instead of participating in complex decisions with wide effects, Moses had nothing to do each day but watch grazing sheep as he pondered how his life had been reduced to this. He became a nobody, going nowhere with nothing. As I read this email lesson I could see on the laptop screen this was more than just a teaching about Moses. Swindoll's devotional was providing a narration of my life. His description of Moses' transition into obscurity was the perfect explanation of my own life at that moment.

Circumstances, orchestrated by God, had moved me to a place of isolation where my daily routine was of interest to no one. The privileges and activities I had enjoyed as a business owner were gone and I was barely getting by in a subsistence lifestyle that supplied nothing more than the basics of life. According to Swindoll's teaching, this was God's plan. In a modern day version of the Moses' exile story, I was living in God's school of life and this course was called Obscurity 101. Swindoll explained the importance of this foundational lesson.

If you would graduate from (God's) school of the desert, you must take classes in obscurity; it is the first required course of the school. If you don't learn to live peacefully with obscurity, you will repeat that course until you do. You cannot skip this one and still graduate.

© 2016 Chuck Swindoll, Insight for Living Ministries

Obscurity was the perfect description for my life. The exile of the oil field had been clear but until this moment I didn't have a term or an understanding for the subsequent trucking assignments I had lived through. Reading Chuck's teaching I understood, for the first time, that this was not chaos, nor was it bad luck and it wasn't punishment. God was working out a personalized, individual plan for my life that was better than any plan I could assemble on my own. My modern day wilderness was being lived in the cab of a truck weaving back and forth across the entire United States highway system. Moses had herded sheep and I was herding trucks. No one out here had the slightest interest in who I was or what I had ever done. I was obscure. For several minutes I sat in that truck on the edge of a huge truck stop in Virginia and wept. A flood of emotions poured forth as I processed the realization of how God was transforming me from the inside out. For the first time in this multi-year experience I understood that God was using this trucking wilderness to shred my misguided, secular understanding of the purpose of life.

A message on my cell phone advised that the broker had made my daily pay deposit and money was available on my charge card. I drove up to the fuel island and bought thirty five dollars of diesel fuel to get the truck to Pottstown along with another cup of bad coffee and a truck stop breakfast sandwich. I had plenty to ponder as I pulled onto Interstate 81 going north through the Shenandoah Valley, one of the most beautiful drives in America.

The following day, Chuck Swindoll expanded my understanding as his email teaching series continued to examine Moses in the wilderness. Chuck explained how God uses the various conditions of a wilderness experience to break through the layers of protective resistance life builds around our hearts. Initially formed as a protective barrier against the pain of life, these layers of resistance build up until they prevent God from molding us into who we need to be.

Obscurity, Chuck explained, is one of God's tools that works like sandpaper to gently remove layers of built up pride. After peeling away our pride, God uses life challenges, to expose our inner fears, past present and future, and then teaches us to trust Him and defy those fears. As we release our fears by trusting God we begin to see that He is always in control even when life appears to be chaos. Working through this process, God uses solitude, experienced during a period of isolation, to break through the bitterness and resentments we accumulate over time. In the long, quiet periods of isolation, we are encouraged to let go of expectations that give us a false idea of what life should be.

Within the depths of a wilderness, after breaking our barriers and re-writing our beliefs, God uses discomfort and struggle to remove the innermost shell of our resistance opening up a path for Him to renew our very core.

Swindoll's emails reminded me that I was not the first to experience God's training through a wilderness struggle.

Randall L. Cumley

Jesus walked through the desert first. He felt its heat. He endured its loneliness. He accepted its obscurity. He faced down Satan himself while the desert winds howled. And you can be sure He will never, ever forget or forsake the one who follows Him across the sand.

© 2016 Chuck Swindoll, Insight for Living Ministries

Over the next two months, Swindoll's daily devotional series directed a spotlight into my own personal journey of the past three and half years. Each day a new email from Insight for Living provided details about a wilderness education. It was as if the series had been written specifically for me. Leaning on the masterful teaching of these podcasts I could fully see God's work in the lives of His people through history while examining my own life in parallel.

In early May I set out on a truck delivery with a yellow box truck being moved from Denver to Portland. This was a beautiful ride through the Rocky Mountains, across Idaho and then beside the Columbia River through Oregon. A last-minute change of plans just as I delivered the truck forced me to scramble and change direction. When the Uber driver picked me up I was hustling to the Portland airport to try and catch a flight to Phoenix where a heavy duty flatbed was waiting to be moved to Denver. The Portland airport was not far from where I had dropped the box truck but I was trying to make a tight connection time. While discussing with the Uber driver what security at the Portland airport might be like, my phone rang and the screen displayed the number of the truck moving broker. He needed me in Seattle the next day for a truck that was a high priority customer. The Uber driver flipped around and we headed to the Amtrak station.

Riding Amtrak in the evening from Portland to Seattle was very enjoyable. As soon as the train was rolling I relaxed with a sandwich and soda in the dining car and then spread out my laptop and briefcase. Completing my trip paperwork on a table instead of a truck seat was a rare privilege. Amazed at today's technology, I connected my smartphone to the Wi-Fi on board the train and faxed my delivery documents to the broker. Then, with my tiny suitcase in tow, I moved to an assigned seat where I kicked off my shoes and curled up in a pair of roomy train seats for a much needed nap.

At the downtown Seattle train station I used the Uber app again, to summon a friendly driver who drove me to another fifty dollar motel in an old section of downtown Everett, Washington. The reservation had been made online through my smartphone over the Internet service on the train. The loyalty points I had accumulated with this motel chain in recent weeks got me this room at half price. When the Uber driver dropped me in the parking lot at midnight I looked over the outside of the motel and wondered if twenty-five dollars had been overpriced.

Fortunately, the interior of the room was better than the outside had suggested. My alarm was set to start another day in barely six hours. Deep sleep overpowered the city noises from the street outside allowing me to wake feeling rested. The nap on the train had helped. As the sun rose that morning I left the room key on the dresser and pulled the door of the motel room closed behind me. I stepped into a dreary, overcast and damp morning. Crossing a wide downtown street before rush hour traffic had started, my tiny suitcase in tow, I ducked into a convenience store to get cash from an ATM. The twenty dollar bill that came out needed to be broken into smaller bills since my travels today would be on public buses. I bought a cup of coffee and asked the clerk for the change in singles.

There was a light mist in the cool morning air as I walked three blocks to a downtown bus station. The small bag rolling along behind me was showing the wear and dirt from too many trips in the past six weeks. This small, simple suitcase, purchased at a thrift store for four dollars, was already worn enough to be a throw away when I bought it three years ago. In my previous life, where I traveled to Belize frequently, I was always carrying personal items to give to the locals. Things they could not get in a third world country. My trips to Belize would involve a full suitcase but then I had to pay luggage charges to bring the empty suitcase back. I decided to find a bag I could carry to Belize and throw away. For some reason, the bag went to Belize but wound up coming back with me. It was the perfect size for this current Trucking-Uber-Airplane adventure where I had to travel light and avoid luggage charges.

I was wearing dirty jeans with a hooded sweatshirt and towing my well-worn four dollar suitcase when I joined the other bus riders in line to buy a ticket. My ego silently told my mind, "You look just like one of 'those' people." My mind understood what my ego was saying with the phrase "those people." I looked exactly like the homeless and poor people who populate downtown bus stations at 6:30 a.m. This was not the home of the rich or privileged and it was certainly not the lifestyle of the American Dream. In the next nanosecond my mind retaliated at my ego by retorting that I not only looked like "those people," I am "those people." This really was my life. This was a long, long way from the successful American businessman I used to see in the mirror.

Exile: A Modern Wilderness Journey

With a three dollar ticket in my sweatshirt pocket I sat on a damp bench to wait for my bus. The Styrofoam cup of convenience store coffee warmed my hands as my thoughts reviewed Swindoll's devotional series about Moses in the wilderness. My understanding of the story was that God had held Moses out there for forty years which seemed like a really long time. Subconsciously I was worried how that might translate to my own, very real and very current, wilderness lessons. Silently fearing He might be planning to keep me in the wilderness longer than I wanted to be, I asked God, "Did you really have to keep Moses out there for forty years?" In his typical nanosecond response God grabbed my attention with only four words: "*It's taken you thirty.*"

That statement caused my entire adult life to flash through my mind so fast I was surprised I didn't spill my coffee. Four words just summarized my own life and at the same time brought in a completely new understanding of Moses. That gave me plenty of thoughts to process on the bus ride north. What I had just been told, in typical God style, was volumes of teaching condensed down to four words.

He was saying first off that Moses didn't stay out in the wilderness all that time because of God's schedule. Moses was out there because of his own stubbornness, bitterness and tough heart. Moses did not have Chuck Swindoll to break his life down and read it back to him. My mind envisioned Moses herding sheep in the desert of Midian alternating his thoughts between anger over being run out of Egypt and bewilderment at being abandoned so far from civilization. Moses had been raised in the palace enjoying the finest life Egypt could offer before he became a fugitive hiding from society. I couldn't ignore a comparison to my life of money and privilege as a business owner now turned into a vagabond moving from truck to truck in dirty clothes. Just as Moses' choices, decisions and actions threw him from royalty to obscurity, my own behavior, I realized, is why I have become nobody going nowhere. God didn't keep Moses in the wilderness for forty years. Moses held himself in the desert by not recognizing the need to change his heart.

I immediately understood, and could clearly see, that my adult life had been cycling like a carousel around one business after another. Pride had pushed me to achieve but it also hardened my independence. When life kicked me, like it had several times, I failed to see that God was trying to get my attention. Instead of turning to Him in those difficult times I had pulled myself up, declared my determination and renewed my fight against the challenges of life.

When times were hard I did my best to recruit God into my plans but I never grasped the concept of following His plan. In the times when success began to appear, I took the credit and forgot about God. Never in the process did I understand that seeking, finding and following God's plan would have been the correct response. The response that would have led me out of the wilderness I didn't realize I was in. In all of those years I had been chasing the wrong definition of success. I had spent my adult life surrounded by the Bible but I had adopted for myself precious little of the wisdom presented. Instead, I had willingly joined the noise and distraction of striving to win the rat race while pretending to be a follower of Christ. My own stubbornness had held me in a self-created wilderness for more than three decades even as I was surrounded by God's calling that could have led me to a life of freedom.

The truck I picked up north of Everett was going to Dallas and the route would include an overnight stop at home in Colorado. That gave me two days to process this revelation before sharing it with Mary. When I got to the destination I found the truck was a nearly new Peterbilt sleeper with every luxury and option a trucker could hope for. This would be a sweet ride to Dallas complete with a fantastic stereo that connected via Bluetooth to my phone. With the cruise control set at seventy and praise music filling the cab, I had a lot to think about.

Mary and I usually work together on a jigsaw puzzle in the middle of our Colorado winters when the weather holds us inside for several days at a time. We have a process we always follow. Find the edge pieces first since they are easy to spot. Once the border pieces are all in place we sort the rest of the puzzle pieces into piles based on color or design. We find something that makes a group of pieces similar and bring those into a working section. Eventually, the groups and sections find their place in the big picture and then we find those unique pieces that tie it all together.

The bus station revelation from God about Moses was one of those unique pieces in my life puzzle that brought the segments together revealing a bigger picture. I was now more than three years into an intense journey that started with my questioning life in the heat and hard work of Belize. God had worked slowly through practical life lessons to reveal and assemble different components of the puzzle which answered my questions from Belize and, in the process, applied those answers directly to my life.

The following week I made another crazy *"move the trucks"* run that took me from Denver to Baltimore to Florida to Houston to the Texas/Mexico border and back to Denver. Three trucks, one airplane, one rental car, four Uber drivers and a Greyhound bus carried me more than five thousand miles over six days. When I dropped the last truck at a dealer in Denver the last Uber took me to the light rail train for a ride to the Denver airport where I caught a plane to Belize.

The guest house I had enjoyed so much in Belize had been sold and I had to move my personal belongings over to my unfinished house. The new owners did not need me for housesitting like the previous owners had. My phone rang while I was standing at the Denver dealership waiting for Uber. A man I had worked with back in the highway construction business was calling to recruit me. His company had a new client and needed employees to service the contract. Kevin thought of me and found my phone number to see if I would be interested. He had no idea what I had been through the past three years. When I returned from a quick four-day trip to Belize I interviewed for this job that would pay better than the trucks and would keep me home every night.

Kevin's company offered me the job to start in two weeks. I made one more truck moving trip during that time to keep the income flowing. That final trip was as chaotic and miserable as they all had been ending with an all-night drive across Oregon and California in another bobtail day cab. The trip ended in Sacramento where I caught a flight home, gratefully knowing I would not have to move another truck.

EPILOGUE

Over a three and a half year journey through a chaotic wilderness God had broken my pride, erased my identity, and brought me to my knees to be entirely dependent on Him down to every daily detail. He did this in direct response to my plea for understanding and meaning in life.

In the heat and hard work of Belize, I had asked God to show me why humans struggle through our short lives in toil. He responded by enrolling me in a training school I didn't know existed. God removed from my life the distractions of a consumer society and allowed me to focus on a message that had been in front of me, but I had ignored, overlooked and marginalized for decades.

That three-year period which I initially viewed as humiliating and frustrating and possibly even a life setback was actually God's inspired answer to my own prayer asking Him to show me His truth.

I have come to understand that our time on this planet is an intentional journey of personal choices that will both reveal and reshape who we are as individuals. Our most important goal in the short time we are allowed to be here should be to find and get on the narrow path that leads to the narrow gate of Heaven. Our eternal soul is developed through the process of negotiating that narrow path.

Watching the workers in Belize struggle through life with a complete lack of both assets and opportunity initially confused me. I was measuring their life against a modern, western, first world standard of affluence, assets and leisure as signs of success. It was a very limited, very worldly, viewpoint. When my own affluence had been stripped away I faced the question again but from an entirely new perspective. Fortunately, in the process of trimming my life to this new reality, God had graciously provided teachers presenting Biblical truth in a way that broke through to my previously distracted brain.

I am now fully convinced that success in this life is not defined by collecting assets, establishing a life of leisure or achieving a financial plan that carries our flesh to the grave. Contrary to popular opinion I have to state that the adage from the eighties about he who has the most toys wins is more than just false, it is an eternal disaster. Equally destructive to our eternity is the idea that a life of comfort, ease and security is a display of success. Pursuing these as a goal in our lives hinders God's attempts to shape us using His tools of challenge, struggle and isolation.

I am not proposing that wealth or leisure or assets are in themselves an impediment to eternal success. God may provide wealth and comfort to whomever He chooses and they may employ those gifts in the pursuit of Kingdom work. I am, however, confident that pursuing and seeking and working to obtain earthly comforts as our primary goal distracts us from the true reason we walk this planet at the start of our personal eternity.

Exile: A Modern Wilderness Journey

The brief time that we will each live in this realm will determine the course of our life for a far, far greater time in the next realm. We have been given an opportunity to determine our own eternity and too many of us have pushed that opportunity off as an item on some future to do list.

This life is only a success if it places us onto the narrow path that leads to an eternity in God's presence. Any accomplishment or task or activity that does not support a journey into a successful eternity is a distraction that defeats the real reason we are here.

If our hearts are set on achieving earthly goals we will miss the opportunity to walk forever as a companion to our Creator. Jesus told us the highway to destruction is wide and many are on it. The path to heaven, where we will commune daily in the perfect love of God, is narrow and few will find it. I don't want to be so distracted by the process of accomplishing secular goals, amassing worldly assets or enjoying earthly pleasures that I fail to find that narrow path. I do not want to trade away an eternity of perfection just to receive a century of folly.